Hyperconnectivity

Computing and Connected Society Set

coordinated by
Dominique Carré and Geneviève Vidal

Volume 3

Hyperconnectivity

*Economical, Social and
Environmental Challenges*

Dominique Carré
Geneviève Vidal

WILEY

First published 2018 in Great Britain and the United States by ISTE Ltd and John Wiley & Sons, Inc.

ISTE Ltd
27-37 St George's Road
London SW19 4EU
UK

www.iste.co.uk

John Wiley & Sons, Inc.
111 River Street
Hoboken, NJ 07030
USA

www.wiley.com

Library of Congress Control Number: 2018951169

British Library Cataloguing-in-Publication Data
A CIP record for this book is available from the British Library
ISBN 978-1-78630-087-4

Contents

Introduction

In the first volume of the series "Computing and Connected Society", André Vitalis uses a sociohistorical approach to question *the uncertain digital revolution*, 50 years of computerization, by taking a closer look at the four main social issues which progressively arose from society turning towards IT and from the development of IT applications: social control, security, commercialization, data exchange and communication.

In the second volume of this series, Laurent Gayard studies the rise of the *darknet* where, unlike the Internet, anonymity is the rule and the identity and location of the user can be concealed, which throws into question the capability of State bodies or market players to set up effective monitoring of the Internet. This desire to escape institutional control responds to ideological and illegal motives and also, most unexpectedly, increasingly economic motives. It promises, sometimes falsely, a globalized system where all borders, boundaries and regulations are obsolete.

The third volume of this series returns to communication and data exchange in order to address the matter of hyperconnectivity brought about by a multi-faceted digital

The authors would like to thank Safir Mimene for proofreading the text.

proposal which relies on relational practices as much from companies, governments, groups and communities as from citizens and individuals. Picking up again on the question of data exchange, of interlinking, this volume proposes an analysis of the reasons for this hyperconnectivity from a communication point of view, and to identify its consequences as much on the economy and society as on the environment. The uniqueness of this approach concerns the issues above all viewed through the prism of communicational and relational practices. Focusing on these inevitably leads us to address the opportunities and uses of what is known as Digital Information and Communication Technologies (DICT), signs of a social acceptance of data mining, since the users now emerge as actors and contributors to this hyperconnectivity. Very often the driving force of a socio-economic model based on indirect financing through free access, hyperconnectivity affects the social practices and environmental issues of billions of people worldwide. In fact, in 2018, DICT have become part of our daily lives and are at the core of everything we do, even the most intimate things. Gérard Berry says that "the world is becoming digital". Digitalization plays such a part in our lives, we could say that "online" and "offline" are mixed in our everyday lives (Berry, 2008), so much so that social practices have been technologized and technology has been socialized. As we will see, the main feature of implementing current DICT is to break the users' fascination with IT, or even the network players' enthrallment to "virtualism". The purpose is no longer to take people to a virtual world which cuts them off from others and society, but to immerse them in a social environment where, on the contrary, those who do not approve of the digital injunction are excluded. Online sociability sometimes replaces, but above all complements, extends and enhances more traditional interactions, while redesigning them, as Antonio Casilli points out (Casilli, 2010).

It should be noted although that for some users, this relationship is so intense, so addictive, that without an Internet connection they are like orphans, helpless and deprived. As a report by the World Bank points out[1], it is worth keeping in mind that while in the so-called developing countries, the diffusion of cell phones – the favorite tool to connect to digital services – is faster than access to water, only 31% of the population of these countries are connected to the Internet and 60% of the world population remains excluded from the use of digital services.

What makes the exercise difficult is that DICT are ambivalent and paradoxical. They are ambivalent as they can contribute to emancipation and freedom of speech and action, but also to subjection, confined alienation[2] and control. They are paradoxical as they can power a production and exchange system which relies on the communication industry, but its economy relies on practices that are essential for maintaining this system.

Therefore, the analysis of the industrial offer in technical and economic terms, which brings with it diverse remote services and relationships, identifies a socio-economic model that relies on three elements: no cost, financing through advertising and data sales, and constant requests in favor of hyperconnectivity. This generates significant changes in creating links by changing or supplementing social practices with a friendly, cultural or professional vision. However, digital communicative practices have an impact on environmental issues which are too often ignored.

---

1 World Bank's Digital Dividends Report 2016, available at: http://www. Worldbank.org/wdr2016.
2 Alienation is limited if we are referring to tension autonomy, or even the "creative capacity of communications and information" (Lefèbvre, 1981, pp. 143–144) and forms of alienation, as demonstrated by Henri Lefebvre (1981).

The analysis of a social acceptance of usage data exploitation, which is not a response to an offer, helps us to understand the tension surrounding the users during their experience. In fact, they supply information by negotiating their use while becoming actors of hyperconnectivity, backed by constant innovation. Therefore, the content generated by users and algorithms orchestrates hyperconnectivity, which spreads in all socio-professional groups. This approach challenges the analyses which most often present the strengths and/or the dangers of hyperconnectivity.

The analysis of social acceptability of the computerization of society does not prevent considering the meaning of uses in the framework of a negotiated renunciation. In the context of the uniformization of consent, a contemporary sociality appears alongside environmental risks and injunctions.

Before presenting how this volume is composed, it should be noted that it is based on a number of research projects conducted over several years by the authors on the theme of "Innovations in communication: devices, standards and uses" at the Laboratories of Information and Communication Sciences (LabSIC) of the University Paris 13 – University Sorbonne Paris Cité, as well as their activities with the Association of teachers and researchers CREIS-Terminal (IT and Society Research and Teaching Coordination Center and journal *Terminal*). This explains the high number of sources from the authors of this volume that the reader will find in the bibliography.

Chapter 1 presents the context of hyperactivity through the establishment by the communications industry of a mass offering of diverse and customized services which promotes monopolistic situations and hegemony.

Chapter 2 analyzes the economy of hyperactivity which is based on free access; two methods of indirect funding, advertising and data sales; and an activation mode, the constant request. They all create an unmatched situation of social control. As for the government, its role is to support and boost the digital economy.

Chapter 3 deals with the ownership of digital technologies and social acceptability of usage data exploitation.

Chapter 4 deals with negotiated renunciation in digital environments, with algorithms which target generalized traceability.

Chapter 5, dedicated to environmental issues, aims to demonstrate that production-driven technologized relational and communicational practices impact on electricity consumption and on the production of greenhouse gases which are a source of global warming and climate change.

Finally, the reader is invited to enhance their reflection with a few perspectives on this ongoing phase of intensive social computerization to address the social, relational and environmental unsustainability of hyperconnectivity and the unprecedented spread of digital information and communication technologies which oscillates between emancipation, solicitation, injunction and subordination.

1

The Technological Offer
and Globalized Services

Considering the anteriority of the offer and the fact that without a technological offer there is no usage, it is important to clarify how a technological offer accompanied by a range of different services has gradually been designed and globally established in a very short time. Alongside this consideration of the anteriority of the offer, it must be acknowledged that devices deployed by some users are increasingly present, and the offer does not necessarily mean usage, sometimes it even feeds on social innovations, such as free software or common digital dynamics. It is not about retracing the development of IT which, despite what some literature may say, did not develop without interruption, linearly and without failures. The development of IT since World War II has not been a bed of roses[1].

It is useful, by referring to volume 1 of this series "Computing and Connected Society", to reconsider some features which have brought about the evolution of an important phase of social computerization which: the implementation of the network of Internet networks. Both the founding technical specifications and the discursive

---

1 In France, the Antiope system illustrates this well. See (Carré, 1994).

productions it brought can be identified in order to understand the development of the offer and its spread over a longer timescale. Similarly, it is important to mention the values which still exist today, such as freedom of expression, sharing and free and universal access, which have somewhat faded or are mixed with more contemporary values. They can be found in the orientations and usage within the guidelines proposed not by simple operators, but by genuine communication giants operating on a global level.

1.1. Importance of the open communication protocol

It is estimated that four time periods have passed since computing began. Each period was influenced by a type of dominant technology, but not only, without having prevented the evolution of other technologies or having substituted some of them, leading each time to new opportunities that are integrated in a social and economic logic and in the strategies of the main actors. Four periods can be identified. The first one was dedicated to hardware; the second, to software; the third, to the network; and the fourth, the current one, to data. This can be illustrated using two examples. It can be said that the Internet would never have been this important in connecting if access equipment such as smartphones did not exist. There is no doubt that miniaturization, the integration of many features on the same hardware, the autonomy provided by batteries, not to mention the decline in prices and the personal ownership of connection devices (which are no longer the property of a family) have strongly contributed to a daily, recurring, mobile Internet usage[2]. It is the same for *apps*[3] (app stores) which,

---

2 It was the same for the wireless radio which belonged to the household then, thanks to miniaturization, became portable and personal. It is the same for computers (micro-computers, notebooks, tablets).

3 It was Apple who launched this type of application in 2008 with its on-line app store (*Widgets*) for the iPhone.

from a smartphone and without a Web browser, allow direct access to a wide range of content, most of the time for free, on every continent.

As everyone knows, the Internet was born in the United States in 1969 when the ARPA (Advanced Research Project Agency) decided to link its main research centers to share resources, exchange data, and to maintain a communication system in the event of an attack on American territory. The establishment of this network was the result of a study carried out in the early 1960s by the US Air Force which concluded that there was a need to move away from centralized IT architecture, considered too fragile, to design a decentralized meshed network architecture able to remain functional even in the event of partial destruction of the network by enemy forces. With the American army abandoning this network at the beginning of the 1980s, it was given to the National Science Foundation (NSF) and made available to European research centers to promote the establishment of cooperative links between research communities. It was only at the beginning of the 1990s that the Internet was gradually opened to companies and private individuals.

Three technical innovations were to greatly promote its deployment, particularly to the general public:

1) The development of the Web (World Wide Web) that enabled publishing and consulting documents through the Internet via a Web browser.

2) The creation of a multimedia system with a client–server architecture.

3) The implementation of high bandwidth networks facilitating high speed.

In 1995, the Director of Research at INRIA, Christian Huitema, stated:

"None of us would have imagined being concerned with sales or invoices. The network was certainly expensive, but not more than other equipment, supercomputers or particle accelerators, that the community made available to the researchers for free. It was only to be used 'at best' to advance science." (Huitema, 1995, p. 8)

As for Patrice Flichy, he indicated in 2001 that:

"For nearly 20 years, the Internet has developed outside the market economy. Free access and cooperation were at the heart of this Internet user culture and market trading was even banned. But, little by little, a new commercial and economic discourse emerged on the network systems." (Flichy, 2001, p. 223)

Thus, after being deployed for the military[4], then among the higher education and research community, the Internet was opened to businesses and gradually since the mid-1990s to the public so that they could search and gather information (via the WWW: World Wide Web, which is based on a system of hyperlinks), access software frequently free of charge (*freeware* or *shareware*), exchange files, and especially – and this is what will be particularly interesting here – connect and communicate (electronic mail, mailing lists, digital social networks, etc.) whether it is on a professional, commercial, administrative or even personal level, while freeing us from the constraints of distance and

---

4 As were many information and communication technologies, even before they became digital. For example: the telegraph, radio communication, the computer, GPS, among others.

time. Meanwhile, since 2010, the Internet of Things has been spreading, whether in the domestic, professional or leisure spheres. The things, identified and connected, rely on the users' data and location, via various interfaces from which they can communicate. Therefore, mobile Internet uses allow you to think about environments, incorporating networks, applications, goods and services in daily life from which all types of actors, human and non-human, communicate and produce data.

The Internet of Things, also called Web 3.0, is developing in parallel to the Data Web and the Semantic Web, and relies on the interoperability of networks and diverse connecting machines, thus promoting the monitoring of all types of activities. This relies on the basis of the Internet, that is, the dual communication protocol TCP-IP. Its undeniable originality comes from the fact that it is an open protocol which is not dependent on a computer company. This is a common language which allows each station or platform to communicate with all the others. Accessing this global network requires hardware (computer, laptop, digital tablet, smartphone, etc.) and a broadband connection. New actors, the ISPs – Internet Service Providers – provide the Internet connection. Specialized companies or traditional telecommunication operators are able to offer this service which is often accompanied by additional services.

Experts, preachers and gurus of all kinds say that Internet diffusion relied on the following assumption: the global network was going to eliminate intermediaries by encouraging direct connection between individuals, an individual and an organization, or a seller and a buyer, etc. Over 30 years later, it is obvious that nothing of the sort has happened. Instead, more often new actors, who are called infomediaries, control mediations and are more and more powerful especially as the technical systems provide many opportunities to be achieved in a personalized way, with a maximum number of people in the least amount of time, regardless of the geographic range.

This situation contributes to a process of globalization of trades and services which differs from the more traditional internationalization process. The devices tend to align at a global level to offer messaging services, search engines, digital social networks, e-commerce, connection, video sharing, etc. even if usage differences exist or persist depending on the cultural spheres.

Obviously, the aim is to think of a global governance[5], not only on a technical level, so that the TCP-IP can evolve and respond to a global demand of IP addresses, but also in terms of political and geopolitical issues between countries and pressure groups to co-regulate the Internet. Is this path going against the initial design of a network of networks, for "personal freedom", which has contributed to its social ownership, as Patrice Flichy (2001, p. 223) indicated, or according to Fred Turner[6]? Above all, it is about promoting the dominance of information and communication flows with the evolution of the protocol TCP-IP. The Electronic Privacy Information Center points to a "threat to confidentiality and anonymity"[7]. Monitoring is largely at play on

---

5 Available at: http://www.voxinternet.org/. See the final research program report supported by the National Research Agency in France, ANR-Voxinternet: c2so.free.fr/report_final_Vox_Internet.pdf. See also Massit-Folléa Françoise, "Uses and Governance of the Internet: for a Socio-political Convergence," in Vidal Geneviève (ed.), *The Sociology of Uses: Continuation and Transformations*, pp. 153–178, Hermes Lavoisier, Paris, 2012.
6 Fred Turner, *From Counterculture to Cyberculture: Stewart Brand, the Whole Earth Network, and the Rise of Digital Utopianism,* p. 396, C&F Editions, Caen, 2012.
7 From 2004, available at: http://epic.org/privacy/Internet/IPv6_comments. pdf.

digital networks, but it would now intervene at the very infrastructure level of the Internet, yet without preventing social, legal and scientific innovation maintaining on-line performance as an open and emancipating network.

1.2. Mediation and industrialization of connection

We no longer only interact with tools, objects, scattered techniques or even machines, but with an interlacing of technical configurations interconnected with each other, running 24 hours a day, all year round and often made available by the servers of companies specialized in storage, (*data mining*), electronic mail hosting services, application hosting (software becoming an online service), blogs, websites and digital platforms hosted most of the time in what are called *Data Centers*.

Companies leading this market offer cloud computing services to their SaaS customers (Software as a Service); in this configuration, the software is installed on remote servers rather than on the user's machine or to IaaS customers (Information as a Service). Experts believe that the market is worth approximately $150 billion and still growing fast.

It should be noted that the main operator is a subsidiary of Amazon, Amazon Web Service (AWS) which holds 33% of market shares globally (source: Synergy Search)[8]. This activity is much more profitable than its e-commerce activity. In 2016, the *cloud* represented a little less than 9% of Amazon's total turnover, but 75% of its consolidated result, or $3.1 billion (source: Amazon's annual report).

---

8 Google, Microsoft and IBM hold approximately 20% of market shares. One of the only French and European actors existing at the global level is OVH.

We are no longer only faced with the arrangement of technical objects, but with a complex interlacement of the most diverse technologies, which constitute "devices" of mediation, to use the Foucauldian terminology[9]. The characteristic of mediation[10] is that it implies the idea of an intermediary, a third element, which is introduced in the relationship and enables the connection of individuals who would otherwise have never met. Socio-technical devices, which are not strictly technical but also include discursive productions, institutions, rules and meaning creation, register these in a time dimension necessary to understand social issues, as Michel Foucault points out[11]. According to Josiane Jouët (1993), they develop:

"Around a double mediation [...] at the same time technical, because the tool used structures practice, but there is also a social dimension, because mobiles, the forms of use and the meaning given to the practice are replenished in society."

In 2011, she underlined the value of *Internet studies* (Jouët, 2011, pp. 45–90) for taking into account the explosion of online services and of new interfaces, thus reconfiguring the users' relation with time and territories while also renewing a communicational action within social practices.

---

9 See the writings of Michel Foucault: 1975, 1976–1979, 1994.

10 For more information on the question of the temporality of mediation devices, refer to (Lamy and Square, 2017).

11 Within the Foucauldian approach, Giorgio Agamben develops a more radical approach. He defines the device as "everything that has, in one way or another, the ability to capture, guide, identify, intercept, shape, check and ensure the gestures, behavior, opinions and discourses of living beings." *Qu'est-ce qu'un dispositif ?*, p. 80, Rivages, Paris, 2007.

These technologies undoubtedly play an essential role in the globalization of trade, in two ways as Félix Paoletti mentioned: as a sector with globalized activities and as a sector producing infrastructure which supports the globalization of activities in other sectors (Paoletti, 2003, pp. 43–45). He states that the network promotes trade globalization, because:

> "Globalization is not limited to the creation and development of networks of multinational enterprises, of global networks of electronic business, trade or financial transactions and stockbroking. The ambition of the proponents of globalization goes much further: globalized companies must be able to spread their activities on a worldwide scale, without any constraint, in financial areas as well as in stock markets, in production and marketing of material goods and services. Moreover, the proponents of globalization think that all human activities as well as the products of these activities should become merchandise that can be bought and sold on this worldwide market."

To spread activities across the globe, usually a new type of company appeared with infomediation as a function. Infomediation is about connecting a supplier (of goods or services) with a buyer. The main manufacturers are known under two acronyms: GAFAM (Google, Apple, Facebook, Amazon, Microsoft) and NATU (Netflix, Airbnb, Tesla, Uber). Many of these newcomers have developed a strategy about encouraging a disruption, that is, challenging conventions, regulations, existing socio-economic models, or even the market itself. How can the success of these newcomers be explained? By setting up an innovative technico-organizational device conducive to the disappearance of entry barriers in a business sector or in a market. Airbnb and Uber illustrate this method very well.

The large mass of users, the considerable volume of connections on a daily basis, the huge quantity of data processed, the multiplication of diversified processes, the rise in power of usage and the effects of usage mean that in order to be able to offer diverse and increasingly personalized services on a worldwide scale, operating all year-round, communication companies have to rationalize, automate, specialize functions, standardize formats and substitute labor with capital; in short, they have to industrialize the connection, strengthening as well as extending the industrialization process to an activity which was deprived of it. As an illustration, Facebook, currently the largest social media network in the world, has almost two billion accounts of which more than 30 million are in France alone. In terms of requests: 30,000 billion pages have been indexed by Google and 20 billion sites are crawled (visited) per day[12]. As for YouTube, the video sharing site, there are more than 1 billion active users on a monthly basis. In France, the visitors are estimated at 4 million unique visitors per day. 2/3 users go on this platform several times a day and 2/3 have access to YouTube from their smartphones[13]. What emerges is an immense technological power, never reached before, to process all these connections and data. The increase in power can be seen at the very heart of the technical process; as for the magnitude, it relates to the abundance of uses.

---

12 Source: *Business Insider*.
13 Source: YouTube, November 2016.

1.3. Monopolies and dominance

Power and greatness depend more and more on the communication industrialists GAFAM and NATU who embody, as David Fayon notes, USA's global supremacy, not to say hegemony, in the digital arena and on the entire value chain: hardware, software and data[14].

Remember that in the beginning, Google was only a simple search engine. Since then, Google has become a subsidiary of Alphabet and is much more than a search engine today, as it is also an operating system for smartphones (Android), a document storing and editing tool (Drive), an Internet browser (Google Chrome), an e-mail client (Gmail), a geolocation app (Google Maps), a social media network (Google+), a video-sharing network (YouTube) and many other services geared towards advertising, as Chapter 2 will show. As for the quantitative data collected on this industrial group, they are frightening. They would own more than 900,000 servers, and in November 2016, Google's world market share in the field of search engines was 92.9%, Bing 2.7% and Yahoo 2.2% (source: *StatCounter*[15]). In 2015, Alphabet had a financial result of $74.5 billion and an annual profit of $23.4 billion (source: Alphabet, 2016). Undeniably, this Internet industrial group holds a dominant position on a global scale, even if it is only in certain geographic areas, as is the case in Russia where it holds only 49.97% of market shares, followed closely by the Russian search engine Yandex (45%), in South Korea where Google only represents 62.22 % of market shares, and in China where it has only 2% of the market, whereas the Chinese search engine Baidu holds more than 78%.

---

14 Keeping in mind the importance of IBM, Intel, Cisco and many start-ups, see (Fayon, 2017).
15 It is worth noting that, in Europe, the market share is 93% and in France, it is 94.1%.

If we extend our analysis to the ranking of Web-based companies, in the top ten, seven are American (e-commerce, search engine, social media network, travel, video on demand), and three are Chinese (e-commerce, search engine, social media network). The first European company comes sixteenth, the German company Zalando (e-commerce). BlaBlaCar, the French start-up world leader of long-distance carpooling, with more than 20 million users spread in 20 countries, is very far behind. It should be noted that this start-up is not the source of this application software which was created in 2006 via the free website covoiturage.fr. BlaBlaCar acquired this site which was stagnating when renewing the connection processes between drivers and passengers.

The hegemony does not stop there: to better realize its importance, it is necessary to identify the location of the Internet's root servers (highly strategic servers). Following research, ten are set up in the United States, two in Europe and only one in Asia. This demonstrates how the United States of America with GAFAM and NATU dominates the world market except for a few geographical areas, as seen earlier.

In this context, France and Europe play a less significant part. By way of example, on the IaaS market (*public cloud*), France and Europe are absent. The United States dominates the world market with: AWS (Amazon), Google, Azure (Microsoft) and, to a lesser extent, IBM. Only China seems to be able to withstand American hegemony even if it is only in its own territory and in Southeast Asia for the moment[16].

---

16 As David Fayon states, *op. cit.*, p. 175. China's strategy was built in three stages: 2003, filtering and blocking of unwanted foreign sites took place; 2006, a parallel system to the Web, to manage domain names with, was instituted, along with the formalization of censorship by keywords; and finally "sinicized" Web tools emerged: Baidu (in place of Google), Youku (modeled on YouTube) and Renren (which is like Facebook).

This country has understood the strategic importance of IaaS infrastructures. As proof, the Aliyun company (Alibaba Group) massively invests in this type of infrastructure and is beginning to spread overseas. China has developed its own "GAFAM", the BATX: Baidu, Alibaba, Tencent and Xiaomi.

By analyzing the setup of data centers, it shows that the large majority are also located in North America. Focusing only on the 24 largest cloud operators on a global level, 45 data centers are located in the United States, eight in China, seven in Japan, five in the United Kingdom, four in Australia and four in Canada (source: Synergy Research, 2016).

North-American hegemony raises a tricky question about the digital sovereignty of our infrastructures, our connections, our data storage and our processing. What would happen to a country that does not master the technological devices being used? What could happen to data in the event of a serious crisis? Understandably, this raises another question, that of collective and public security, since personal data (including names) is "sensitive" data enabling direct identification, and increasingly even in an indirect way, of any physical person[17] via the digital traces (connection IP address, navigation trails, geolocation, etc.). Some even give access to information on the habits of Internet users. This collection of personal information is usually done without the users' knowledge. Therefore, it is of the utmost importance to question these terms, because, where the data is stored or processed, with few exceptions, the law of the country that hosts the servers applies.

---

17 Such as the name, date of birth, social security number, genetic fingerprint, and also a vehicle registration document, debit card statement, among others.

How can the hegemony of the United States be explained? There are several factors to consider.

First, it has a capacity to innovate and master innovation in a general manner and digital innovation in particular. For example, Google owes its success to its search engine which incorporates an innovative algorithm: PageRank, an information filing system. When a document is pointed to by many hyperlinks, its PageRank increases, and the higher it gets, the higher the probability of being displayed in the first ten results of a research. According to Dominique Cardon, this system gives an indication of the "authority" of the document among the other documents on the Web. Therefore, the more a site is listed by others, the more weight its recognition of others has in the calculation of authority. This method, as the author recalls, borrows

> "from the system of values of the scientific community, particularly from the scientific reviews rankings which give more weight to the articles most cited by others [...] this recognition measurement has greatly proved that it is one of the best approximations of the quality of information." (Cardon, 2015, p. 26)

All this is governed by an algorithm and by a business model which is based both on the promotion of keyword advertising via AdWords AdSense and on the principle of the auction for advertisers. This manufacturer keeps innovating. The latest innovation is to interconnect all the services offered by Google with the aim of analyzing the activity of any author regardless of the application and possible promotion of the website connected to the Google account in the search engine results. Netflix, a media provider that offers films and series on demand or by subscription whatever the connection medium (television, smartphone, tablet, computer, game console), also derives its success from the development of an algorithm, but this one predicts the tastes of the spectators from automated learning (machine learning) of the traces left by Internet users on the site in order to better advise the viewer on their future choices. It is the same with Amazon which has developed a predictive technique that can make purchase recommendations. Most sites, particularly in e-commerce, use algorithms of recommendation based on comments, notes, likes and similar profiles.

All these connection industrialists give an important place to innovation and have developed sophisticated algorithms to establish themselves in a particular activity. Algorithm design is becoming strategic and necessary and allows a company to become established in a business sector.

Algorithms are not a recent innovation, but their links with big data and global networks, their sophistication and the place that they hold, give them today a capital importance because they are able to operate at very high speed, using huge amounts of data, to prioritize information, guess what we are interested in and select what we prefer. To paraphrase Dominique Cardon a little, we could say that we manufacture algorithms but in return they build us up (Cardon, 2015, p. 7). Digital technology is definitely an absolutely essential tool to standardize calculations and quantification, but for this author:

> "Since the neo-liberal policies of the 1980s, we have witnessed a generalization of calculability and a systemization of the benchmark policy. The presence of quantifiers in social life is felt everywhere. Barometers, indices and charts start to put numbers on activities which, until then, were not measured or for which quantification was not the object of constant attention." (Cardon, 2015, p. 9)

Next, to understand American hegemony, we must consider the capacity of economic actors to integrate "the network effect". The digital world has a low tolerance for competition, due to a "law" of its own. The premise can be summed up as follows: the utility of a good or service grows with the number of users; hence, the importance of very quickly acquiring a mass of users so as to be in a dominant position over competitors. This generates exclusivity in the market. In this case, as the economists point out, *the winner takes all*. Thus, there is also the necessity to acquire innovation very quickly instead of developing it in-house while acquiring expertise and offsetting any potential competition[18]. That is what GAFAM and NATU did. Therefore, monopolies are created and the main emerging feature is that the acquired companies become part of the buyer's offer while still existing autonomously. This is the case, for example, with LinkedIn and Skype (Microsoft), or YouTube and DoubleClick (Google). This tendency is certainly not new, this process of acquisition, of concentration, although in different forms, had already been identified by Patrice Flichy[19]. In the 1970s and 1980s, the electronics industry went, in 20 years, from a largely competitive market to an oligopolistic market. This trend had been thwarted in France by the government which at the time set limits on this concentration or nationalized the sector. The same concentration can be seen in the sectors producing cultural goods. What about the famous "two hundred audio-visual families within French capitalism"? And as this author always indicates, is it not widely known that cultural industries have "two centers of the World: Hollywood and Sony City?"[20].

---

18 It should be noted that Google has purchased more than 150 companies, as of today.

19 See *The industries of the imagination. For a socio-economic analysis of the media*, p. 38, PUG, Grenoble, 1991.

20 *Ibid.*, refer more particularly to Chapters 7, 8 and 9.

Hegemony can be explained by the capacity of American start-ups to mobilize venture capital and make a stock market valuation. Take the case of Uber. The last fund-raising campaign raised $68 billion while this company, since its creation, has reported a loss of over $5 billion. Does this seem beyond understanding? Not for digital start-ups. Actually, investors gamble on the future by taking a risk. They do not rely on financial results, but on the forecasts of future profits. In a way, they bet on the ability of a start-up to be the future world leader of an activity. In Uber's case: booking a car with driver. Fund-raising is tied to a business strategy which aims to gain market shares as quickly as possible, since the hallmark of the digital economy, as seen before, is the network effect. In fact, the only assets Uber has are its app, its brand and its market shares. It should be noted that some specialists begin to wonder if unicorns (start-ups with a value exceeding a billion dollars) are not overestimated and fear a financial bubble[21].

To conclude, it is necessary to remember the infomediaries' ability to establish their dominance by providing a free service that allows them to value the uses thanks to the multitude of data they collect and sell. According to David Fayon, if we summarize his remarks, web firms usually use two main logics[22]: the *leader* logic, which is the ability of an actor to become dominant in a new market, and then to monetize their audience, even if it means waiting years after launching the offer on the market to reap the benefits. Google illustrates this perfectly. The logic of the *ecosystem* is the ability of an actor to develop a flagship application which then becomes a platform while offering open APIs (an interface that ensures the interoperability of applications) to attract a community of developers – and volunteers if possible – who will offer

21 This is the case, for example, of Will Gornall and Illya Strebulaev (2017).
22 Fayon, 2017, pp. 47–48.

services that rely on the platform, while taking advantage of
the data provided by Internet users. Alibaba has adopted
this approach. Offering its first application to its home
market, this Chinese company has developed what is called
an "ecosystem of comprehensive services" to extend its grip
on other markets in order to keep hold of the maximum
number of users. It is a double strategy: offering many
services for free or at a very low cost to attract the greatest
number of users, and encouraging developers to propose new
applications and services while enriching the platform of this
communications giant.

American hegemony is reinforced by the fact that the big
companies usually practice tax optimization while
exonerating themselves from any participation in content
financing: this greatly improves their profit but weakens
some public policies. This happened to existing cultural
policies. Like other platforms, Uber uses a mechanism of tax
optimization, which is called, in this case, the "Dutch
sandwich". Payments are channeled through the
Netherlands, then through different tax havens, thus largely
evading tax. It should also be pointed out that it bypasses
social rules, does not pay for a license and offers carpooling
services which evade regulation. According to the European
Commission, tax fraud and evasion costs the European
Union €1,000 billion in tax revenues (a large part of which is
from digital technologies). This is equivalent to the entire
health expenses of the member countries of the European
Union. It should be noted that the European Commission
has recently ordered American firm Google to pay a fine of
€2.42 billion for abusing their dominant position. This
sanction was imposed after a seven-year investigation. The
multinational was reproached for promoting its price
comparator "Google shopping" in the search engine results,
thereby penalizing other actors in the sector. However, the
Commission's services also focus on other activities,
particularly its online advertising platform AdSense and its

mobile operating system Android, also for abuse of a dominant position. We should emphasize that France and Germany have just taken a joint initiative at European level to obtain taxation of all GAFAM platforms and other pure players[23].

The technical offer associated with a multitude of services, as seen before, is involved in the technologization of social and professional life, especially as Internet users can communicate at any time, in any place and are able to publish instantly what they want to share, reaffirming the practices of writing and reading. It is important to remember that what has been called Web 2.0 (also called participatory and contributory Web) is not, contrary to a widespread or advocated idea, a new innovative technique that would replace Web 1.0. Indeed, when physicist Tim Berners-Lee invented the Web, this possibility existed. However, it is the rise of bandwidth and the spread of broadband that blessed the participatory and contributory direction. From a technical point of view, there has not been a second Web generation, even if this term has strongly contributed to promoting a Web orientation.

With this global network of exchanges and communication functioning 24 hours a day, year-round, undeniably the question of the irreversibility of the use of these socio-technological devices no longer seems relevant, since they bring anything, anytime, anywhere, on any device. Hyperconnectivity makes digital disconnection impossible and even if the situation may give rise to criticism, digital injunction creates conditions of non-disconnection, all the more so when Web 3.0 is spreading, which relies on the semanticization of data (called the semantic Web, based particularly on the qualification of data and its

---

23 The case of Airbnb is enlightening. In 2016, this platform only paid €92,944 in France, even though it is the second largest Airbnb market in the world.

categorization) and the Internet of Things (each object having an IP address). Moreover, users' skills allow them to escape as much as possible the grasp of their devices, to avoid being permanently under injunction, nonetheless without disconnecting. Therefore, a question arises: how can we explain the rapid success and diffusion of a technical offer associated with connection services of communication companies on a global scale? This will be covered in Chapter 2.

The Hyperconnected Economy

The global success of connection services by computer and telecommunication networks is explained by the free nature of this network of networks. With the Internet, everything is free, or almost free... Some start from the principle that Internet users pay with their time, the time they spend browsing to access content. While we must clarify, as it will be seen below, many nuances and while the cost-free factor is important, it is not sufficient to explain a massive and globalized diffusion in such a short time. The attractiveness of uses should also be considered: it cannot be denied that the seduction and appeal of the services offered encourage interactivity and auto-production of the most diverse content ("user generated content"). Hence, every Internet user can be both a receiver and a transmitter; they are capable of designing, publishing and even editing content. This also explains this success, not to mention the significant and unprecedented proliferation of amateur content. To fully appreciate this mass diffusion, we need to shed light on the underlying socioeconomic model. The proposed approach considers that it is necessary to remember the role of *Homo economicus*, while taking *Homo socius* and

Homo communicus seriously, which is not the case in most economic approaches. We believe that the combination of three factors contributes to the functioning of this model of connection: a mode of access and use, two modes of indirect funding and a mode of activation by request. These modes will now be analyzed, one by one.

2.1. A free mode of access and use

Free access is associated with most applications, and most content available on the Internet, to such a point that the term "free access economy" was coined. For Chris Anderson, the reason is that any Internet activity has almost no production or (especially) distribution costs. "The new industrial revolution"[1] would come from this tendency. Jeremy Rifkin perceives, in the emergence of *the new society with zero marginal cost,* a way to eclipse capitalism[2]. While it is true that the production and distribution costs are almost zero, it is not certain, as Rifkin claims, that this will eclipse capitalism. Actually, the opposite assumption could be made, that nowadays free access is at the heart of capitalism and could strengthen it, or at least guide it toward new forms.

If applications, services and in many cases content are free for the end user, they must invest in the purchase of a device (micro-computer, notebook, tablet, smartphone, etc.), to access it and take out a contract with a telecommunication operator who provides Internet access. If it seems free to the end user, it is because the cost does not depend on the time spent using it, but more often on a package. There is therefore no single billing which reflects the number of connections and the time spent on the network.

---

1 For more information, refer to the book *Makers: The New Industrial Revolution*, by Chris Anderson (Pearson, 2012).

2 The exact title is: *The Zero Marginal Cost Society: The Internet of Things, the Collaborative Commons, and the Eclipse of Capitalism* published in 2016 by Babel.

Free access in the digital universe will become important to the point of becoming the norm. Is this an unusual situation? Has there been any precedent? And if so, when did this free access emerge? This section will attempt to answer these questions.

First of all, it is useful to recall that the Internet developed, as seen previously, outside of the market economy. As Patrice Flichy rightly points out, with free access and cooperation at the heart of Internet culture, market exchange was prohibited. Richard Barbrook even stressed the "anarcho-communist" character of this network (Barbrook, 2000, pp. 55–76). For a long time, as Flichy (2001, p. 223) points out, free Internet access did not give rise to debate; it went without saying:

> "Some IT professionals who bathed [...] in the tradition of university's openness and freedom were the first to theorize, in the 1980s, the principles of cooperation and exchange which were the basis of the Internet. Their thinking was to initiate the free software utopia, laying the foundations for an alternative economic theory".

In this context, resistance movements against certain entrepreneurial and mercantile deviations began to emerge and sought to protect software through patent application or legal measures. The free software movement illustrates this perfectly. By making source codes available, hackers opposed the exclusive ownership of software by computer companies. Other movements were based on the principle that information had to be free and shared by all. The development of Wiki[3], an online cooperation tool for web page creation and edition within a group of Internet users (a community), is another example. The free online encyclopedia Wikipedia co-produced by Internet users has

---

3 In Hawaiian, *Wiki* means "quickly".

dealt a fatal blow to traditional encyclopedia publishers. The practice of musical files exchange over "peer-to-peer" (P2P) to promote the circulation of cultural productions are also part of the same line of thinking. Undeniably, the network of networks has been a place of confrontation between the free access logic and the commercial logic. Peer-to-peer could also be regarded among the first darknets[4].

Next, the case of French style telematics should be mentioned. During the 1980s, when mainstream telematics was being rolled out, France Telecom (which was a public authority at the time) gave away free Minitels to households to promote access to paid services offered via Videotex in order to reap financial revenues from the connections. This meant that in 1989, 16% of households had a Minitel and only 8.2% a personal computer[5]. It should be recalled that Teletex access costs depended on the added value of the service (36-13, 36-14, 36-15, etc.), on the distance and on the length of connection. It is the socioeconomic model of the meter which prevailed and not the package subscription. The longer the connection, the higher the cost. By analyzing the diffusion of telematics, Kevin G. Wilson showed, as early as 1988, that with each connection, the operators in return scooped information on the practices and behaviors of individuals. Therefore, in addition to the payment by users of access to telematics services, there was, in addition, the collection of detailed information on the habits and behavior of individuals who used the services[6]. This information could then be used by the companies for marketing purposes or possibly be sold to other service suppliers. This author even considers that the information collected could ensure the

---

4 The reader may refer to Volume 2 of the series "Computer Science and Connected Society" by Laurent Gayard (2017).
5 "Telecommunicating at home", *INSEE first*, no. 137, May 1991, available at: epsilon.insee.fr/jspui/bitstream/1/9996/1/ip137.pdf.
6 For more information, the reader may refer to the work of Kevin G. Wilson (1988).

sustainability and profitability of telematics. This has not been the case in France and in many countries, despite the proactive policy pursued by the French public authorities to promote the development of Videotex publishers and the setting up of databases. The supply has not really met the demand. Videotex in France developed, in fact, around two main applications: information and transactions, and leisure uses (adult chat, games). While the deployment of French telematics has helped encourage the development of a marketing approach, the diffusion of mobile telephony leads then to usage marketing (Carré and Panico, 1997, pp. 241–249). The identification of the uses is then used to facilitate the rapid market entry of new products and services[7]. Since it was hard for telematics to find a mainstream market, the arrival of the Internet put an end to its deployment.

It is important to consider the case of the *SpiralFrog* platform which, in partnership with Universal Music, made a first attempt as early as 2006, offering North American Internet users free access to its musical catalog in exchange for 90 seconds of advertising. In return, the user could download a free piece of music. This was of course a major company's attempt to put an end to the endemic decrease in revenue from CD sales despite the implementation of legal downloads, all the while fighting the exchange of music files via P2P platforms. The approach had attracted other major companies (EMI, Sony BMG, etc.) to fight Napster, the first site to encourage Internet users to share their musical files.

Widening this investigation to the media reveals that radio, television and even the press have used free access on many occasions. This free content provision is carried mainly by advertising revenue. It is a classic, well-known

---

7 Carré and Panico, 1997, pp. 241–249.

funding model in these sectors. In order to give listeners and viewers free access, media outlets sell advertisers the possibility of broadcasting their advertising. The price is determined by the audience level. As for the programs (i.e. the content), according to economist Dallas Smythe, their only purpose is to recruit a potential audience and to keep their attention. This approach has been used and reformulated in a more pragmatic and blunt manner by Patrick Le Lay (The Associates of EIM, 2004); the President Director General of the audiovisual group TF1 indicates: "What we sell to Coca-Cola, is available human brain time..." This model, which was used by private TV and radio stations in the United States of America, was exported during the second half of the 20th Century and became dominant in Europe and beyond. The principle set out by this economist was that in contemporary capitalism, the audience is the product in the area of communications (Smythe, 1977). The aim of a channel is thus to maximize its audience. It is the same in the press for free daily newspapers (*Metro*, *20 Minutes*) distributed or made available in train stations, underground stations or other public spaces.

Finally, it can also be recalled that a significant part of the economy sits in a non-marketing logic (health, education, retirement)[8] although these still involve money because all or part of the price is socialized[9]. In this case, a fixed price is built socially and depends on political, ideological and cultural orientations.

So, free access is not a concept that only emerged with the development of the Internet. This use and access mode is present and has been at the heart of media functioning for decades and, to a lesser extent, in the diffusion of French telematics. Free access grew in importance after the failure

---

8 Even if there is an increase of the commercialization of its activities.
9 Free services, low cost services, or with a price depending on resources, consumption level, or types of use.

of online services marketing in the 1990s as Serge Proulx and Anne Goldenberg (2009) reported. Industrialists gradually transformed many paid services into free services for the user, but paid for by advertising[10] to promote the development of online services. One of the reasons cited by these authors and which is seldom highlighted comes from the system of social exchanges brought about by the Internet. The importance of trading intangible goods reveals the limits of intellectual property laws as applied to the digital universe. Free access is thus part of a double commercial logic. One, using a principle which has made its success with the media: selling advertising space, but with new forms. The other, more innovative logic is to sell personal data (with names) collected from the Internet users, which was sensed as early as the end of the 1980s by Kevin G. Wilson (1988). The usefulness of a connection service is now measured by the number of individuals who use it; the greater the increase in subscribers, the greater its usefulness. Based on this principle, free access then becomes a way to quickly attract new users in order to expand quickly and gain market share. For Mattelart and Vitalis (2014, p. 167):

> "The free services of online businesses are bait to attract the largest number of consumers whose identities and profiles are of interest to advertisers. It is advertising that funds these services which are financed in "currency of life". The hidden face of free access, which will become the dominant economic model on the Internet, is identity piracy".

It should be noted that there has been a trend for some time based on a hybrid business model. The basic services remain free ("freemium"), but sometimes services with a higher added value are offered ("premium") and are thus

---

10 Serge Proulx and Anne Goldberg, 2009.

charged. The example of Skype is emblematic. The service offered allows the user to make free phone calls via the Internet, but it is also possible to pay for additional services such as calls on land lines and mobile phones.

Cost-free, the Internet access and use method is one of the elements that contribute to the construction of a hyperconnectivity economy. The next section will tackle the indirect financing method which in return constitutes a necessary supplement to implement free access.

2.2. Two indirect funding methods: advertising and data marketing

Free access does not in any way mean that trade and commerce logics are absent, but that the notion of free access is strongly entrenched at the very heart of the capitalist system. Michel Gensollen (1999) pointed out that free access to services is "sold". In return, for the introduction of free access and use, two main types of funding[11] will be required: advertising revenue from advertisers (purchase of space, sponsored links, etc.) and the marketing of personal data (with names) collected on the Web (connections made, links clicked, the digital trail of our browsing habits, etc.), thus favoring targeted marketing which is increasingly refined and powerful. The industry is now abandoning usage analysis and are turning to audiences and traffic analyses in order to quantify their return on investment

---

11 If we do not count the marketplaces which do something besides connecting, because they play the role of a trusted third party, guaranteeing the buyer to be delivered and the seller to be paid. For this work a commission for "time and effort" ranging from 10% to 15% is then charged.

(ROI)[12]. These measuring techniques are then used to justify the price of advertising to their clients (the advertisers).

When implementing an advertising system on the Internet (sale of space, banners, etc.) or selling data, the type of algorithm used is crucial, because it will favor a strategic direction that promotes, according to the typology formulated by Dominique Cardon, either popularity (counting the number of clicks to measure the website audience), authority (assessing the hyperlinks shared to establish a meritocratic ranking), reputation (counting the number of "likes" to value people and products) or even prediction (use traces to identify implicit individual behaviors) (Cardon, 2015). Algorithms thus enable us to model individual or collective behaviors to develop marketing approaches, and also, even if this work will not deal with those, detect fraud, assess risk and predict possible or probable events.

As non-specialists in advertising marketing or in online data production and marketing, the following sections modestly aim to give some contextual elements and describe some of the operation rules in order to understand the role of these two indirect financing methods in the constitution of a hyperconnectivity economy.

2.2.1. *Advertising revenues*

The focus will now be on the way communication industrialists sell advertising space. In France, online advertising represented €3.45 billion in 2016 – *Observatoire de l'ePub* (e-Advertising Observatory). For the first time, it surpassed TV advertising. The online sector grossed nearly 29.6% of media investments in 2016, against 28.1% for television. The online sector has allowed advertisers to better

---

12 Carré D., "Etudier les usages. Est-ce encore nécessaire ?", In Vidal G. (ed.), *La sociologie des usages : continuités et transformations*, pp. 63–85, Hermes-Lavoisier, Paris, 2012.

target those they plan to contact, but also to better measure the performance of their campaign and to use approaches encouraging social and cultural homophily ("birds of a feather flock together") among others, all this for costs that are often 10 times lower than those of traditional media (television, written press, radio, billboards, etc.) and for more satisfactory results. Remember that there are two major types of advertising, *search* and *display*. Search is based on the sponsored links that appear in the results displayed in a search. Display refers to offering advertising spaces on websites. Banners, one of the common forms of online advertising, enable the advertiser to prompt the user to click and visit their site. Another approach is to roll out customized marketing in order to build a personalized relationship with each user by sending e-mails, for example. Instead of attracting the users' attention when they go on the sites, they directly receive information according to their interests.

Remember that originally, Google was just a simple search engine. Twenty years later, this communication giant has become both the greatest global online advertising sales agency and an advertising medium via its system of sponsored links. The click and the conversion rate have become measurement units of the effectiveness of Internet advertising campaigns. The most visited sites are ranked monthly. This ranking then determines the value of advertising banners. Specialized companies are even called to "click" so as to increase the visibility of certain sites or activities on the Net. With AdSense, an online advertising application, Google gives websites the possibility to display advertisements on their pages. These are administered and paid per click. Google also offers, for a fee, contextual advertising which is advertising related to the content of a web page and its location. These new advertising systems offer a real-time auction system carried out by algorithms. As described by Dominique Cardon, when a visitor loads the desired web page, their profile is automatically auctioned so that robots programmed by advertisers compete for the best price in order to best place their advertising banners[13]. As for the AdWords system (a keyword advertising system), it assigns a value for keywords with an auction system for advertisers. As far as Facebook is concerned, this digital social network (DSN) giant offers, for example, applications to customize its members' pages. In order to install the applications, it is necessary to give "super friends" access to the most personal data. Otherwise, the installation will not run. The strength of this DSN, and incidentally of others, is to provide a large number of free applications while introducing an advertising format tailored to the information served to users of this network and a purchasing platform for spaces accessible to advertisers. In 2011, Mark Zuckerberg, Facebook's charismatic leader, promised that he would not be like Google: i.e. would not use browsing history to more successfully target advertisements. Three years later, he has reversed his position. Facebook announced that it will use data collected on external sites visited by Internet users to more successfully target the advertising it offers on its network. Of course, there is still a "do not track" function in browsers, but advertisers who use the services of Google and Facebook do not have to honor this.

In response to this incessant flow of advertising, an "attention economy" is developing. This economy relies on the following exchange: Internet users agree to receive offers of services, most often under duress, but also sometimes with a degree of benevolence, it must be recognized, in return for their attention. This is the basis for current marketing strategies. This occurs in the web sector, and according to some economists and specialists, attention is a rare resource in an over-informed environment. "Abundance of information

---

13 Cardon, 2015, p. 49.

creates an attention shortage"[14]. To remedy the situation and stand out from the competition, it is necessary to use strategies to stimulate users' attention. These strategies are above all the responsibility of communication companies and agencies, but also of some individuals such as *Youtubers*.

Note that the pages the user accesses are no longer generic but contain contents and suggestions customized for each user. As for the prices, they also begin to be defined according to the users' interests. This leads Doc Searls (2012) to state that the consumer's freedom of choice becomes mere fiction and it is very far from the principles of free economy. This is why he proposes the implementation of an "economy of intention" so that users, through the use of new tools, can take back control. Note that each advertising invasion occurs most frequently without prior consent. The completed forms, the data transmitted, usually unbeknownst to the user, are the price to pay for free access to a multitude of applications and services. As everyone knows, Facebook has built its business model on the sale of advertising based on the behavior of its users. This well-known discourse is comical coming from this communications giant; Zuckerberg claims to be doing the users a favor by showing them advertising which may be of interest instead of flooding them with spam. All this contributes to what Ivan Illich calls the "shadow work", the unpaid activity of the user, the consumer who gives back a commodity its use value, to use or consume it. It is the shady side of the industrial process (Illich, 1981). It should also be pointed out that Illich uses this expression to describe activities and exchanges that are not part of the monetary sector.

---

14 As pointed out by Simon H.A. (1971). For a more theoretical approach, see Goldhaber M.H. (1997).

2.2.2. *Data production and sales*

Light will now be shed on how data marketing is carried out, but first, it must be retrieved and produced. Starting from the principle that data creates value, Google and Facebook were the very first to see the interest in gathering, processing, using and selling data. As Internet users log in more, and as the audience grows, it becomes easier to harvest and to monetize the data that in return, feed a real industrial chain of data production ("Big Data") and a socioeconomic model that does not escape a questioning of emancipation and social control conditions.

Data gathering is carried out in five ways: recovery of technical log in data (IP address), browsing trail (website cookies), collection of content submitted voluntarily by Internet users (publication on digital social networks), identification of location (geolocation) and finally through completed mandatory forms or questionnaires. In this case, to obtain the answers, companies do not hesitate to give symbolic (or not) rewards, gifts, discounts, etc. The exploitation of the data gathered is carried out via an automated and complex mass processing system ("data mining") to better understand the behaviors, discover the tastes and detect the needs of the consumer in order to offer goods or services likely to be suited to the Internet users themselves. Geolocation, of course, increases these possibilities. Data is becoming the oil of the 21st Century; the organizers of the opening conference of the Big Data exhibition in Paris in 2015 were not mistaken, naming the conference "Data, the oil of the 21st century".

Consider for a moment the cookie, placed by web browsers. In the 1990s, its purpose was to facilitate user navigation. It has now become the advertisers' Trojan horse to "invade the privacy" of every web user, privacy that it spies on at the slightest connection or navigation. The cookie's aim is to capture and supply data on each user.

Remember that some cookies are no longer installed by communication companies, but now mainly by advertising agencies who can supply different advertisers with the data they obtain.

There is no doubt that data trading is expected to increase in the years to come, according to the last Consumer Electronic Show (CES) which was held in 2017 in Las Vegas and which gave the "Internet of Things" a prominent place. What can be said by considering the interest of some people in implementing the practice of *quantified self*, initiated by individuals themselves and paradoxically in two areas, health and well-being, which inherently affects everyone's private life? This new practice is based on automatic capture and personal data sharing modes.

Note, however, that this only concerns active Internet users and to a lesser extent occasional users but not those who do not connect and who are therefore untraceable. They are the weak link of these devices.

So, is this a global process of "informationalization"? This neologism coined by Bernard Miège and Gaëtan Tremblay (1999) is used here to refer to this form of data industrialization, even if, for these two authors, informationalization refers primarily to a wider process which is supposed to describe the correlated phenomena of information and communication, both at production and at distribution level. We attach here a more restrictive scope to this notion to characterize the trend of human activities to become equipped with industrial devices to collect, record and extract information which require analysis, comparison, feedback and regulation information devices to extract social information links which can give rise to social abstractions, which are as manipulable as they are disconnected from society. The purpose of these indicators is not so much to know the reality but, to quote Michel Foucault, "to guide behaviors"[15].

A question arises: is it possible to consider communicational emancipation without falling into economic domination and social subjection since there is, as Henri Lefebvre (1961) pointed out, neither complete alienation, nor complete disalienation as these two components are part of a dialectic movement?

Some try with difficulty. Is condemning a technology enough to make the user break free? There is no certitude here. Those who radically criticize are often the strongest and the most ardent in expressing themselves on the Internet. Some deliberately limit connections in order to limit their digital trail or spend their time configuring their privacy options that these large companies endeavor to change without warning them. Others have decided to resort to the use of search engines which have adopted what might be called an "ethical" position. This is the case for DuckDuckGo or the French search engine Qwant, but these only represent a small proportion of annual searches on French territory, less than 1%. Others install "adblockers"[16], anti-advertising software that can block both "display" ads being loaded and the Internet user's navigation data to avoid "retargeting". The press frequently reports that in Germany and Scandinavian countries, more than 30% of Internet users resort to using adblockers. This trend is significant and is beginning to seriously worry communication companies and advertisers. Internet users with enough technical skills are turning to anonymization[17] or encryption tools, such as Tor

15 Michel Foucault, "The subject and power", *Said and written*, pp. 1041–1062, Gallimard, Paris, 1982.
16 The most well known is Adblock Plus, but a financial agreement has been reached so that advertisements from Google are no longer filtered.
17 For further developments, it is possible to refer to the publication of Chantal Enguehard and Robert Panico (2010).

(the "darknet"), I2P, which both have technology that is less or not identifiable, or use proxy servers. For the moment, this use is far from being accessible to everyone. For this guideline to become significant, as rightly indicated by Laurent Gayard (2017), it would require easier and more attractive navigation on the Tor network, if the goal is to get the general public to use these technical solutions. It is worth noting that, from now on, Tor2Web allows site referencing in .onion in Google. This is an important development to mention. Another way relies of course on practices of a partial or total voluntary disconnection from the Internet: a practice that seems to be increasing. In France, the employees' right to disconnection[18] has been introduced into the Labor Code and came into effect on 1 January 2017. Without going into too much detail, this right to disconnection imposes an obligation on the employer to regulate the use of digital tools within the company. It was introduced in order to impose rest time and leave for employees. It must be brought into effect in the framework of a negotiation; if the negotiation does not succeed, it is necessary to draft a legal charter for the right to disconnection.

2.3. An activation method: solicitation

Free access, as we have seen, is one factor that contributes to building a hyperconnectivity economy. Financing through advertising and selling data thus becomes indispensable. It can be argued that a central and essential third element is missing in order to make a system that works well daily in the long term. It is the integration of an activation mode which is based on important relational solicitation and, if possible, uninterrupted productivist prompts. Instead of the economy of "attention" or the

---

18 Article 55 of Act No. 2016-1088 of 8 August 2016, called Labor law. The right to disconnection for employees appears in article 2242-8 no. 7 of the Labor Code.

economy of "intent", this work would rather promote an approach that is located between production and reception, the economy of "solicitation". This next section will try to sketch an outline of the framework in which it fits. This approach seems more relevant to understand the operation of the socioeconomic model used. This economy is based, above all, on three forms of solicitation. One comes from communication companies, publicists and advertisers, one is used by the most diverse groups or communities, and the last one, which should not be forgotten, which comes from the exchanges between individuals for their professional, cultural, recreational or personal relationships in order to act together.

To account for what is happening on the Net, it is possible to use the Marxist approach. It would rightly be seen as an alienation of the subject and an extension of commercialization, because on this front, the capitalist logic is upfront about its intentions. It has one major drawback: it does not explain the reason of this hyperconnectivity which forces the users to solicit and to be constantly solicited. It seems opportune and above all advisable to explore another equally critical approach, the Foucauldian approach, so as to better address the processes at play between freedom, subjection, expressiveness, social control and data production to understand how neoliberalism, by the importance that it attaches to the "company", would favor this hyperactivity. What does it propose and what does the term "company" cover in this sense?

Keeping in mind the lessons of Michel Foucault (2004) in the courses given on "Security, territory and population and birth of biopolitics" and since this work relies more particularly on the approach proposed by Christian Laval in "L'entreprise comme nouvelle forme de gouvernement. Usages et mésusages de Michel Foucault", we may turn to

Hervé Oulc'hen (2013) summary in the introduction of the same book[19]. He wrote:

> "Foucault sets in this course new foundations for critical thinking, by analyzing neoliberalism no longer essentially as a vision of a world subservient to the fetish of commodities, but primarily as a new art of governing and shaping subjects, a universal "form-company" in all aspects of its existence" (Oulc'hen, 2013, p. 8).

The company must no longer be perceived here as an institution that is a source of wealth, but primarily as a true "social model" which is the basis for the "general form that the company must take" (Laval, 2013). The neoliberal project, Foucault says (according to Laval, p. 148):

> " ... it is not the conformism of consumption, this is not the massification of wage-earning workers, it is the diffusion of the company's form and the implementation of competitive mechanisms at all levels of social relations. What must be brought to light is not so much the passivity of the consumer manipulated by advertising, as the activation of the company man and of the production with conduction devices: "what we are trying to obtain is not a society submitted to goods it is a company subjected to competitive dynamics".

Therefore, relations would be governed by the competitive norm at all levels. From the level of goods and service production to the level of everyday social relationships or friendships, to better steer individuals (Foucault, 2004, p. 154). The individual should be their own entrepreneur. Entrepreneurship is thus an economic force but above all a

---

19 And more specifically, the chapter written by Christian Laval (Oulc'hen, 2013, pp. 143–158).

moral and political form, new regulatory logic with the company as a foundation (Laval, 2013, p. 150). It can particularly be observed in the field of health (Carré and Lacroix, 2001) where neoliberal policies are forcing individuals to be actors of their own health: the focus is on deviant behaviors, the creation of psychological discomfort, the development of a guilt-inducing moral discourse, the diffusion of stigmatizing communication, accompanied by an empowerment of the patient and an outsourcing of care to the family circle (Carré, 2010, pp. 173–182). Everyone, taken individually, must therefore be considered responsible, not to mention accountable, before the nation for the evolution of health expenses. The objective here is to reform and to impose a new operating standard in health (Carré and Lacroix, 2001).

What really pleases individuals is undeniably the modern, appealing nature of DICT and socio-technological devices which make their daily lives easier, therefore offering them the possibility to access services and content freely. But keep in mind that there is also the possibility of seizing new opportunities, meeting new people, fighting inhibitions, reconnecting with forgotten contacts, sharing worries and fears and cultivating similar hopes. Communication companies know this very well. From this social acceptability, of the nature of technology and free access, they acquire the means to individually or collectively solicit Internet users by allowing them to develop or strengthen their affinities and their digital relations. Assuming that community is not antagonistic to trade, they will draw on the founding values of the Internet to stimulate and support the creation of "virtual" communities: individuals who come together and share common interests, without knowing or meeting each other. The objective is to stimulate relational exchanges which have also become mobile.

It has become difficult to resist the irrepressible call, from the moment the primary function – making phone calls with a smartphone – was been supplanted by other features. The smartphone has become a genuine pocket activator on a daily basis, favoring a relational abundance that makes the individual comply with society's expectations that control this ritual. The assiduousness of connection shown by the individuals relies on the following triptych: connectivity, interactivity and reactivity. Undoubtedly, connective technology is involved in and intensifies an increase in the pace of life, as analyzed by Hartmunt Rosa (2010, p. 87), by the increase in the number of episodes of activity and or experiences per time unit, an increase that this author links to the reduction of temporal resources and of the sense of urgency (immediacy, reactivity) that results from it.

The individual, more and more imprisoned by the coercion to connect and communicate, becomes entrenched in an Internet system which allows them to be empowered or at least to express themselves, all the while being profiled. The user is indeed at the same time the user of a technology and the whole component element of the system, by their own contribution, produced by the socio-technological devices. In the last century, every individual was expected to work, produce and procreate in order to make our industrial and capitalist society grow. Today, the multitude is requested to be connected at all times, to share and communicate unhindered in order to feed the networks and to submit to the surveillance necessary to maintain the security of a neoliberal society.

By staying graciously connected, receiving a continuous stream on their smartphones or through other media, users are in permanent contact with different types of devices. Communication channels and marketing strategies then multiply to create a constant, omnipresent solicitation, not to say a relational oversolicitation which applies a permanent communicational pressure. Advertisements, opinions, advice, recommendations, games, appraisals and requirements of any kind from the communication industrialists, advertisers, Youtubers, professional colleagues and friends and potentially any individual are all at hand, offering unprecedented opportunities to connect with non-institutional actors and a certain power of action. The extensive connection of Internet users is sought to broadcast advertisements, but especially to stimulate the production of digital trails, data and content essential to feed the system. These productions are then recovered and monitored to replenish the solicitation process. The objective is to offer friendly, professional or commercial requests in an individualized or even personalized way. This allows industrialists in return to amass new trails, to process them via algorithms or in association with machine learning that changes according to the pace of innovations and uses, self-sustaining the system which has become autonomous, so to speak, while making it more efficient (Carré and Panico, 2011, pp. 26–27). Therefore, the users, often without realizing it, freely give out data about their desires, their tastes, and also on their way of life. These data will be used by communication companies to replenish the connection chain. Bear in mind that without this hyperactivity, the socioeconomic model based on the users' data would actually become depleted, without the intensive supply to the system from the Internet users. The economic actors would then have to find other media solutions to maintain the impossible digital disconnection.

This is close to what Foucault (2004) called biopower: a regulatory and standardizing power replacing a power controlled by the right of life and death of a sovereign over his subjects. If, as this author has shown, medicalization was a way of taking over the body, controlling sexuality, thereby producing it, it could be observed that at the time of media coverage, of self-display and self-exposure, the marketing power substitutes this medical power and brings the incessant need to talk about oneself, to show oneself while pretending to no longer acknowledge troubles, but to show the desires, the most intimate, most secret aspirations of the individual:

> "Therefore, from the biopower exerted on life [...] we would come to a more accomplished form of power, a sort of "sociopower" as we call it, which is exerted on the specific social links that every individual holds in their uniqueness and which the marketing of desires aims to enhance, particularly as seen by stimulating the Internet reflex" (Carré and Panico, 2011, p. 28).

"Do not remain anonymous, be seen, stand out, distinguish oneself", these are the main features of the neoliberal social norm which advocates competition and competitiveness as an ideology. Competitive mechanisms can be encountered at every level of social relations. Neoliberalism does not explain everything. It is supplemented by other practices, other values that will strengthen it, in particular exposure. The order of exposure is not unique to the Internet scene; it does not originate from digital social networks. Talk-shows and reality TV shows of the 1980s preceded it. Borrowing from the prevailing mediatic sociocultural model: exposure injunction (including feelings and emotions), self-disclosure, disclosure of intimacy, posing, recognition of singularities, of live experiences. Industrialists and users participate in the promotion of singularities, reconfigure the separation between the intimate and the public and promote a wide variety of rankings (Carré and Panico, 2012, p. 77). However, YouTube is not strictly speaking the web sequel to Star Academy, but it greatly favors self-publicizing and especially the relation to others on the new social scene that is the Internet[20]. Realizing this ideal of an individual, a freelancer who is sensible, who must distinguish him or herself at all

---

20 As Dominique Carré and Robert Panico noted (2012, pp. 269–283).

costs, stands out from the crowd in order to exist and fulfill themselves.

This technified and mediatized relational opulence shapes an instrumental rationality, a world in permanent connection, where any withdrawal, any time off, would not only be impossible, but unthinkable. A world where new rituals impose themselves, such as always being connected, continuously checking the presence of others, contacting each other even late at night (Carré and Panico, 2013, pp. 177–197).

Through these rituals, the behaviors and the actions generated by the daily use of devices, the neoliberal society never ceases to assert its control on individuals by progressively establishing an operational standard and an increasingly strict social control. Foucault's originality and importance, according to Didier Lapeyronnie (2013, pp. 227–228), comes from a key observation:

> " ... in our liberal and democratic societies, power does not come from one central device, it does not act as a repressive force, it spreads throughout the social space, it becomes immanent and eventually identifies with the categories of social practice. It arises thus from below and from everywhere. Therefore, behind the instrumental rationality, we have to identify the power systems which really organize social life [...]. Power comes from standardization and engages all of society in an indefinite consolidation strategy. The social figure or the individual are not working towards their emancipation, but rather by building themselves or thinking themselves, they contribute to the social functioning and therefore to strengthening the power system".

There is then a weakening of the legislature and of the regulatory framework, as it can be seen in terms of respect of the personal data collected or when implementing disruptive strategies, and there is also a dissemination of power in mechanisms that are more and more reticular, strategic and tactical, spanning the entire social space. With power being no longer, or at least not only, embodied in institutions, there is an establishment, to quote Lapeyronnie, of a "government of individualization"[21].

From a different approach and analyzing *Governance by Numbers*, Alain Supiot (2015) comes to quite solid conclusions. The reason of power, according to him, is no longer sought in a sovereign authority transcending society, but in intrinsic rules for its own functioning. Borne by the uncertain digital revolution, this new institutional imagination comes from a society where law has given way to agenda and legislation has given way to control.

2.4. The government's involvement

What is the role of the government in this unprecedented relational configuration? The goal here is not to analyze what the government does to implement techniques to observe, monitor and deploy activities in the field of data mining, recording the population or in national or global surveillance[22] by listening to and intercepting exchanges to spy on the population or to ensure public security; it is to look at the configuration relating to the exploitation of digital trails, data and content resulting from self-exposure, self-disclosure, from connections or Internet browsing within an economy of hyperconnectivity.

---

21 Lapeyronnie, 2013, p. 220.
22 Such as the electronic monitoring put in place by the United States and their allies, Great Britain and Canada via the Echelon system, which was later replaced.

Among the data hungry, we find, as we have seen, digital communications companies, advertisers, and publicists, but also the government. Trails, data, and content produced by users on a daily basis to feed the communicational and marketing strategies of communication industrialists also interest the government and its police and intelligence services. As observed earlier, one uses the vast pool of information produced by the other (Carré and Panico, 2011, pp. 17–31) and nothing looks more similar now at the time of the Internet than a CRM (customer relationship management) knowledge database[23], a social forum such as Facebook or a police file. It is possible to know what anyone is doing anywhere, their habits, how they stand with regard to norms, or even ways to act for them and on them. This social control over individuals has become more insidious, particularly as it is always more intrusive and never forgets the slightest deed or gesture, producing countless trails, of which we do not know in the long term to whom they belong and what their intentions are, at the right time, to say about each of us from the moment this surveillance is embedded in our most ordinary daily activities. And even though one person out of two deemed themselves worried about the tracking of Internet users' practices, all agree to view this as the price to pay for their unconditional presence in this space of global exchange that the Internet has become (Carré and Panico, 2012, pp. 61–79). Even when there are protests that grow into organized boycotts, against Facebook for example, when companies change their confidentiality settings or when Internet users discover the sale of sensitive personal data considered unacceptable, what happens then? While some abandon this network for a while, few really disengage. Actually, there were more than two billion individuals connected to this digital social network in 2017,

---

23 A CRM gathers all the marketing or support systems or operations with the aim of optimizing the quality of the customer relationship, of securing loyalty and maximizing the revenue or the margin per customer.

with 33 million active users in France alone[24]. This is quite significant and helps understand its appeal. The "kill switch" (interruption of traffic) technique used by governments, in addition to the fact that it may appear drastic, and not very democratic, is usually less effective than it seems, because information services cut themselves off from essential information.

After the collapse of the Soviet Bloc, the rise in power of globalization, the rise of terrorism and the erosion of borders, it has become possible to measure the cost of remote management for individuals in a world without borders. Recording information is no longer sufficient. The need for responsiveness is becoming stronger, and it seems necessary to develop surveillance, the strength of which is to be diffused to such an extent that it goes unseen, invisible to the individuals who are at the same time its impetus and its object. This strengthens the government's network surveillance justified by the globalization of trade, the international political situations and terrorist threats.

This social control is based on a triple register: not to appear in principle as discriminant, not target a particular group; not to look like control by constraint and thus be only very slightly visible, gathering here and there what has already been said spontaneously; while making the ordinary person the subject of this control, or as it were the activator of this control (Carré and Panico, 2012, pp. 269–283). Another question could also be asked, if the walls dedicated to self-exposure on social media networks would not actually be, in the field of information, surveillance and social control, and because of the practices of spontaneous disclosure that they encourage, reward and normalize, more effective now than the strongest police databases or the most hyper-segmented business databases? Since the more active

---

24 Available at: www.lemonde.fr/pixel/article/2017/06/27/facebook-goes-the-BAR-of-2-billion-of-users_5152063_4408996.html.

a user is on the Internet, the more identifiable they become. The cross referencing of gathered data (data mining) and the continuous analysis of behavior and movement (geolocation) ultimately contribute to an intrusive social control and monitoring by companies and advertisers while helping the administrative authorities, but sometimes also individuals.

As recalled by Mattelart and Vitalis (2014, pp. 206–207):

> "It is less a matter of monitoring the whole population than, in a context of free movement of persons and accelerated data processing, of detecting within the feeds of information a population that should be the subject of specific measures. It is not so much repression they are looking for than the anticipation and the neutralization of dangerous behaviors".

And these authors add:

> "Unlike the *panopticon* where one knows they are being monitored and by whom, in the *nonopticon* one never knows if they are being monitored, nor by whom and to what degree of intrusiveness".

To recap, the *Panopticon* is a type of prison architecture proposed by Jeremy Bentham. Its objective is that a guard, housed in a central tower, can observe the prisoners locked up without them knowing if they are being observed. As for the *nonopticon*, it consists of being watched without knowing that someone is watching or at least not knowing to what extent[25].

---

25 For more information, refer to Siva Vaidhyanathan (2008).

The government, as indicated, is not above observing behaviors and collecting data without users' knowledge. It can also intervene and force communications companies to give their data, thus participating in mass surveillance favoring population profiling which is, "a form of indirect control of individuals by using information gathered on them" as Mattelart and Vitalis (2014) pointed out. For these authors, profiling dates back to the employment record book and the first police register. With the Internet, this form of control has kept developing and expanding. In the United States of America, for example, the Homeland Security Act allows authorities to gather any necessary information from Internet service providers. New rules were even adopted in January 2017, allowing the NSA to share private data with other American agencies, without a judicial decision or Congress authorization[26]. And what about Rule 41 which authorizes the FBI to carry out investigations (not to mention hacking) on all digital media, whether it is on American soil or abroad as long as it is considered necessary by a judge? Remember that in 2016, Microsoft refused to hand over e-mails to the American justice service. The reason being that they were stored in France; a land governed by the rules applicable in Europe and not in the United States. It was the same for Apple who refused to deliver the digital key which would have allowed the FBI to access the iPhones[27] of some suspects, thus proving the phone's safety. It is worth noting that demonstrations were held on the west coast to support the position of this manufacturer.

---

26 Members of the European Parliament are concerned and have expressed their fears in a resolution (press release of April 6, 2017).

27 The FBI has requested that Apple agree to modify the operating system of the iPhone in order to enable the authorities to decrypt any encrypted data. The reason is that the security services can compel telecommunication operators to provide access to the data exchanged, but the last generation of iPhones is equipped with a system of fingerprint recognition coupled with a unique coding algorithm for each phone, making it impossible to access data.

European countries have not been idle. In France, the *Commission nationale de l'informatique et des libertés*, CNIL (French National Commission on Informatics and Liberty), ensures compliance with the law and is responsible for preventing any deviation[28]. This law dates back to 1978, but more contemporary laws, like the one on daily security (2001), modified by the 2006 law on the fight against terrorism and others which have followed at an unbridled rate, force Internet Service Providers (ISPs) and telecommunication operators to keep their customers' connection data and to put them at the disposal of the police authorities if necessary. The latest intelligence laws are very oppressive.

As for the European Courts of Justice, it is attempting, with great difficulty, to suppress this misconduct which is considered worrying. This is reflected in the decision of 17 December 2016, which invalidated Swedish and English legislation that aimed to gather a vast and indiscriminate collection of telecommunication users' data (Foegle, 2017). This reaffirmed prohibition of the mass gathering of metadata and led Amnesty International to say that in the digital era, encryption has become essential to privacy and freedom of expression. Encryption should become a right to protect private life and freedom of expression. The verdict is unequivocal: we have witnessed a weakening of personal data protection even though it erodes civil liberties. This led David Forest (2009, p. 4) to say that

> "[...] the society of surveillance is part of a twofold movement of deregulation encouraged by European policies to benefit market laws and police over-regulation".

---

28 Obligation to provide information, duration of data retention, the purpose of processing, consent of the person for gathering, possible recourses.

If the police are monitoring users, with all the smartphones and the DSNs in circulation, it is likely that they will now also be monitored by the same potentially monitored users. The change in status from being monitored to being the monitor was called "underveillance" by Steve Mann (2003). Therefore, monitoring no longer only comes from the institutions, communication industrialists and various agencies, but also potentially from any individual. This would require a lengthy discussion, and it is not the subject of the analysis here. If the reader wishes to go further into the direction taken by social control, they can refer to the joined edition of the journals *tic&société* and *Terminal*, "Contrôle social, surveillance et dispositifs numériques" (Carré and Vétois, 2016).

Now that the context of the economy of hyperconnectivity has been defined, it is possible to address its social and environmental issues in three phases: social appropriation (Chapter 3), negotiations at the heart of digital renunciation (Chapter 4) and environmental consequences (Chapter 5).

3

Social Appropriation and Digital Culture

After analyzing the structuring framework of hyperconnectivity in relation to industrial supply strategies and the mobilization of relational practices based on the socioeconomic model of incessant solicitation, we analyze the social acceptability of the exploitation of data. The latter goes beyond receiving or responding to offers, as some digital uses make sense in everyday life. Users are the providers of their data not only by voluntarily delivering them through procedures and forms, but also by expressing their sociability, with full or partial awareness of the technical capabilities of their exploitation. Hyperconnectivity is supported by permanent innovation causing instability and a variation of uses, whereas appropriation is a long-term process creating new uses from everyday practices. Constant innovation corresponds to the socioeconomic dynamics that keeps the uses operational and arranges them with interfaces of changing interactive modalities that structure the practices of communication, content distribution and consumption for internalization of the standards of digital expressions for a digital habitus.

To consider such a situation emanating from an adjustment to the communication activity, which aims to define reciprocal behaviors recognized by acting subjects[1], it is necessary to define in particular the uses of these *interactive* digital technologies. It is thus necessary to analyze a new form of diffusion that brings users to experience and innovations, in the context of relations that are broadcast by networks, tracked and calculated, and a political and economic organization of the digital transformation of all social activities. Would this be a new form of subordination by negotiated renunciation (Vidal, 2010)?

Could this be a new form of servuction (Eiglier and Langeard, 1987) going beyond the teleservices mobilized by users, exasperated by restrictive ergonomics, revealing the prescribed device[2], apparently without injunction, in short a prescription accepted as a new legitimate criticism to guide, give advice and recommend? In order to grasp the tension between renunciation and negotiation (Chapter 4) of hyperconnectivity implemented by a process of industrialization of digital mediations and practices, this chapter will cover the process of contemporary appropriation of digital environments participating in the formation of a digital culture.

The uses of digital information and communication technologies (DICT) are at the heart of social, economic, cultural and political activities, in terms of both acceptance and social innovation. The uses thus fit into practices opening up to a digital culture in formation and expansion. Still diffuse, digital culture is understood as social appropriation, which means that it concerns all the actors of society, from citizens – regardless of their condition, because

---

1 We may refer to Jürgen Habermas (1973, p. 22).
2 Work used in particular concerning the device: Michel Foucault (1975, pp. 228–264); Giorgio Agamben (2007); Geneviève Jacquinot-Delaunay and Laurence Monnoyer (1999).

even if some do not have digital access, the exclusion criterion now relies on the acquisition of a digital culture – to governments, through economic actors. In a context of intensive digitalization of society, with the deployment of algorithmic data processing, digital culture is drawn from the model of computer networks and of the Internet in particular, also in mobility, with technologies to compute and trace social and economic activities in interacting practices. Digital practices, however, should not be thought of according to an exclusively technological determinism, since tools and instruments do not determine our living conditions, although technological innovations have never been so invasive. It is thus necessary to consider the stakes relating to digital practices under digital injunction, insofar as the techniques employed exert on the one hand a permanent pressure and on the other hand an exploitation by the actors of the behavior of the users who legitimize this pressure. These issues affect economic and political strategies, creating the conditions for social acceptability of digital traceability to reach relational services and technologies.

Digital culture, which underlies all activities, is anchored in a digital society, following the phrase "information society" of the 1990s and 2000s[3], which accompanies the extension of the exploitation of data flows, including files, to process, in the cloud and with connected objects as well, the expressions and social interactions. In other words, this *information* society has prepared the flows, now exploited in a *digital* society. From then on, the digital paradigm penetrates all types of mediation and rules, organizing domination without the need for tyranny, by exploitation and calculation of traces and attention by recommendation with variable legitimacy.

---

3 "Industries culturelles et "société de l'information"", *Sciences de la société*, no. 40, February 1997; "En finir avec la "société de l'information"?", *Tic et Société*, vol. 2, no. 2, 2008, available at: https://ticetsociete.revues.org/497; Nicholas Garnham, "La théorie de la société de l'information en tant qu'idéologie : une critique", *Réseaux*, vol. 18, no. 101, 2000, pp. 53–91.

In regard to digital networks, prescription relies on algorithm-based strategies, which will define the value to be attributed to goods (and services) that will in turn be released to the receivers of prescriptions who willingly discredit themselves as actors by calling on a third-party "prescriber"[4]. The prescription also relies on data from users who are increasingly willing to deliver them to access (often free of charge) online services. The recommendation and ambassador figure, who circulates information, opinions and advice, stimulating exchanges and criticisms on digital social networks in particular, as well as user-generated content, engage in digital prescriptive activities. It is necessary to keep in mind the value of data in regard to a market, which extends through a network of delegations and competences, in other words, a prescription market, linked to the delegation (at least in part) of a decision-making process by facilitators, human and non-human, including community managers, online peers and algorithms.

The selection process, to value an offer likely to meet expectations oriented toward free services or not, can be found in all types of contexts – social, organizational, political, economic and cultural – circulating knowledge, "a ranking, a hierarchy or a list of solutions (or results) ... (from) qualitative or quantitative criteria"[5]. Nevertheless,

---

4 Following the work of Benghozi and Paris (2003, p. 6 and 205–227), which are based on the audiovisual sector, we propose to draw parallels with algorithms, available online: https://halshs.archives-ouvertes.fr/hal-00262496/document.

5 From Benghozi and Paris (2007, pp. 291–310), we note, in particular, that the Internet economy has paved "the way to new market structures by putting forward a prescription function that is clearly distinct from the functions of market offer on the one hand, of logistical functions and the provision of goods on the other hand". The authors state that "the analysis of prescription functions and procedures provides a better understanding of the business models and competitive structures at work in the Internet economy organized around the articulation of three markets: primary goods, referencing, prescription. This modeling of prescription markets

differences are to be noted, when users discuss cultural prescription for example, in mediation and communication devices, by providing an analysis, an opinion on the quality of a work, an exhibition, activities or access to culture.

The concept of mediation, the current meaning of which refers to the figure of the legitimate intermediary to establish an understanding, goes beyond notions of access, reception, transmission and diffusion, since the interfaces of mediation open upon social interactions. Mediation refers to the appropriation that opens up to meaning, through individual and collective connection. Mediation also refers to relationships with the world via the devices that support it. In fact, the relationships between humans and machines, which establish an approach requiring instructions and rules of use at the heart of the device that prescribes these relationships, give rise to power relations between strategies and tactics (Certeau, 1990), in the context of the digital economy based on massively collected and exploited data.

In such a context, digital culture, which is based on the programmed obsolescence of technologies and on stimulation and solicitations of the active participation of the users, in short the hyperconnectivity required to maintain the services with their data processed by the algorithms, opens on prescribed practices. Research on uses contributes to understanding the extent of the situation.

Works on the uses of information and communication technologies (before their digital qualification) in France, included in a sociology of uses (Chambat, 1994, pp. 249–270, Jouët, 2000, pp. 487–521), have multiplied since the 1980s both to understand the social issues related to technical innovations and to meet the production needs of the

---

helps to enrich the understanding of value chains and business relations that can be found on the Internet."

computer[6], telecommunications and media industries[7]. The field of research on uses has produced knowledge on the social appropriation of technological innovations, on the insertion of new uses in pre-existing practices, on their meaning as well as on use circumvention and inventions of use. This knowledge was produced according to a research position considering the uses as an additional activity to other social activities. However, current hyperconnectivity leads to the adoption of a different research stance on digital uses in all social activities on a daily basis.

The figure of the receiver, which evolved during the 20th Century, moved from a receiver who submitted to received messages to a hyperactor, a user figure endowed with a power of opposition and negotiation in a relationship with the issuer, adapting the content according to their cultural interpretation and their power of participation and publication. In a concrete relationship with technologies that are primarily present in the form of objects, from a technological culture, users develop practices, representations and imagination associated with the notions of efficiency and performance, which contribute to their appropriation and a limited form of contemporary alienation. Indeed, this alienation, which covers the impossibility of changing the course of our lives, without the possibility of inventing, is only partial, in a movement of alienation/disalienation, as Henri Lefebvre points out (1961, p. 209 and 211). Even if companies take into account or even use the inventions of the users, these show circumvention and adaptations of uses. The uses of the

---

6 The French National Center for Telecommunication Studies (CNET) and the General Direction of Telecommunication (DGT), in particular, have financed a large number of works.

7 Did these actors dominating the digital socioeconomy know exactly what they would do with the knowledge produced? These studies had to play a role in coping with the telematics crisis after the peak of Minitel in the 1980s (see Marie Marchand, *La grande aventure du Minitel*, Larousse, Paris, 1987).

current DICTs should then be emancipated[8] partially by the possibility of freeing themselves to a certain extent from the authorities, the first being that of the technological devices themselves. However, the users do not think at all times of the relationship of power at work. In fact, their autonomy is hampered by the procedures of the devices that frame the uses, although they are sometimes undefined, unexpected or even surprising.

Therefore, the analysis of digital uses can reveal what is hidden; it can explore under appearances and thus exceed the descriptive approach, nevertheless necessary, of the actual uses. Indeed, the majority of the current research on digital technologies tends to adhere, sometimes with insufficient discernment of the structuring strategies, to the reassessment of the use and the user actor of all experiences mediated by computers with multiple forms, aiming at an auctorial function at the heart of hypermedia contents, including those related to digital relations. These studies produce analyses of inventions and creativity on the part of the users, actors of a "digital society" universally[9] considered liberating, with a deterministic approach. Nevertheless, specific and even unequal positions between users must not be denied, depending on gender, training, location, handicap, device and connection, especially between users and emitters, even if the users are often emitters in their personal spaces of publication in communicating their subjectivities. Despite a large number of DICT usage studies, it does not seem relevant to think about users in stable use categories. Uncertainty contributes to the

8 By retaining that emancipation "begins when we question the opposition between watching and acting, when we understand that the evidences that structure the relations of saying, seeing and doing belong themselves to the structure of domination and subjection" (Rancière, 2008, 19).

9 However, it is essential not to consider uses outside of a sociocultural context, because there is a similar appropriation of interactive technologies from the digital industry worldwide.

development of strategies based on devices that will limit it and allow a return on investment not only for economic actors, in particular, but also for cultural actors, sustained by policies of support and promotion.

The turning point of the 1980s, which gave rise to numerous field studies whose enthusiasm caused a certain dilution[10], can lead the way, in this second decade of the 21st Century, to critical research on digital uses. Indeed, a retrospective look at the work done so far gives a good grasp of the link between the lack of interest in understanding the meanings of uses, because, according to the dominant argument, and the so-called globalization of digital uses[11] and a sufficient knowledge using statistics, since everyone would be connected, without any possibility of escaping the permanent connection. Therefore, economic actors believe that they can determine online behaviors using users' digital footprints. The offers only need to adapt to actual uses to maneuver their communication innovations based on the users' declared desire for autonomy.

3.1. Ambivalence of uses

This work will put the analysis of DICT uses in perspective, to question the paradigmatic axis that underlies hyperconnectivity, at the heart of an ambivalence of uses.

---

10 Bernard Miège, "Questionnement de la sociologie des usages comme voie privilégiée de l'approche des TIC", AISLF GT13 Congress, Istanbul, Turkey, 2008, available at: http://w3.ugrenoble3.fr/gresec/pagespublic/documents/miege_AISLF.doc.

11 Sociological research rooted in a theoretical lineage of cultural studies (see Mattelart and Neveu, 1996, pp. 11–58), which pays close attention to local cultures and allows cultural interpretations to be considered. This field of study has lost its political content with its dilution, including by resistance studies, identity studies and gender and race studies, also removing its critical potential.

Indeed, since appropriation enables the development of communicational and informational practices, power relations can be discussed. This sociopolitical dimension of the uses is to be considered in the framework of negotiated renunciation, a concept addressed in Chapter 4. When users renounce their liberty of not submitting their data to digital monitoring, they negotiate with the same technologies to resist and invent, reproducing seemingly modifiable power relationships, thanks to interactivity – from ergonomic actions to publication through digital social interactions – which has to be constantly maintained by economic and communication actors. The uses thus enter a process of recovery emanating from digital socioeconomy.

Technology, which is essential for the implementation of such a situation, is not the cardinal issue. The articulation of social, economic and sociopolitical issues leads us to take into account the decision-making mechanisms, while delivering the conditions of free will, at least on the surface. After distancing ourselves from the technological deterministic approach that still often dominates discourses and ideologies, it is also necessary to escape social determinism. However, determinants should not be excluded, so as to make allowance for the interventions and postures of users in technological environments.

According to this non-deterministic position, critical research focuses on strategic issues structuring the socioeconomic and political frameworks that predispose hyperconnectivity. It is thus necessary to analyze, at the same time as uses, socioeconomic and political devices and configurations. The longitudinal approach will be used beyond ethnography[12] for the uses that often deliver very interesting descriptions of the users' actions, in order to analyze the ambivalence of uses, within hyperconnected environments, but it is sometimes based on the ability of some users to invent alternatives to escape from it and establish certain self-determination. The goal is to reject the alternative between describing and interpreting and to believe that it is enough to reveal social "realities" thanks to the statistical data understood as objective. In one case (qualitative) as in the other (quantitative), the position of temporary validation and empirical verification is relevant for analyzing uses (at the micro level) in the context of hyperconnectivity (at the meso level), which is part of the digitalization process of society (at the macro level).

In order to further the reflection on hyperconnectivity through socioeconomic and political prescriptive devices, it is necessary to go beyond the issue of access, as it is treated most of the time using the quantitative approach producing statistical data increasingly mobilized at the expense of qualitative studies and surveys, although they take into account the socioeconomic diffusion of digital technologies in society. Thus, the analysis of the ambivalence of uses, in particular, of interactivity, as interactivity, although this name is less and less mobilized in favor of "user experience", refers to functional activity and relational activity by digital means, is rich in knowledge on hyperconnectivity. In this dynamic, it is also necessary to set aside a hidden functionalism, which is currently significant and adequate to value the uses without questioning them, but only calculated and recorded.

---

12 Without claiming the ethnography of usage, some authors work on "real-life situations" (Hutchins, 1994, p. 452), in some ways overlapping what others call the ethnographic approach, limiting studies to the observation of uses, to question in particular laboratory tests (Hutchins, 1994, p. 453). See also Serge Proulx (1999), available at: http://barthes. ens.fr/atelier/articles/proulx 2000.html.

Indeed, the economic actors of hyperconnectivity benefit from the production of usage studies that do not engage in a reflexive ambition about the intensification of the digital world or in the debate on hyperconnectivity devices.

The characteristics of DICT in the second decade of the 21st Century lead us to rethink the purpose of individualizing technologies, such as computers and smartphones, with convergent properties supporting cultural and communication practices now geolocated, preparation for the Internet of Things. These technologies are omnipresent, mobile and miniaturized, and facilitate personal and professional uses. Their appropriation tends to facilitate the ways of doing things, the tactics of users supposed to rely on a "creative capacity for communications and information" (Lefebvre, 1981, pp. 143–144). However, Lefebvre proposed the following critical analysis: "to affirm (that this creative capacity) increases with their abundance, is a) a postulate; b) which contradicts the history of time, space and social practice; c) which also contradicts the degradation principle of energy, whether massive or fine energies such as informational energy"[13].

Analyzing the ambivalence of uses engages on the path of empiricism to grasp the meanings of uses and the subjectivities, without preventing the critical approach of the simulacra of the media society, the burst of identities, the instrumentalization of interpersonal relations, even intimacy, and the gradual disappearance of the boundaries between public, professional and private spaces. However, a multitude of usage studies mainly focus on economic issues (e-commerce, software and applications market, new forms of

---

13 (Lefebvre, 1981).

"gamification")[14] and organizational issues (with collaborative work or communities of practices for example).[15]

The technical possibilities, with the evolution of the IT, telecommunications and materials markets, followed by the evolution of the content industries, are more important (computer and phone memory for example, bandwidth for telecommunications), and miniaturization of communication devices enables their portability. In addition, the uses of the Internet, based on the acceleration of bandwidth and the dissemination of participatory and contributive sites at the expense of the term interactive sites, of crowdsourcing and digital social networks confirm the intensive connection of users to omnipresent networks. Internet users and mobile phone users, and now smartphone users (following technological convergence) are equipped to access the Internet and display their personal data, as well as publicly reconstruct their social groups, interpersonal communication as well as tastes and desires, thanks to the rise in interoperability that still applies. The ease of publication, organized by communication networks and cultural norms, causes the confusion between diffusion and democratization of uses under the participative–contributory label. Economic productions on the Internet then transform the latter into a

---

14 It is worth mentioning, for example, work upstream and at the moment of a significant change in the social appropriation of the Internet: Alain Rallet, "Commerce électronique ou électronisation du commerce ?", *Réseaux*, no. 106, pp.17–72, 2001, available at: http://www.cairn.info/ article.php?ID_REVUE=RES&ID_NUMPUBLIE=RES_106&ID_ARTICLE =RES_106_0017; see for example Serge Tisseron, "Jeux vidéo : entre nouvelle culture et séductions de la dyade numérique", *Psychotropes*, vol. 15, pp. 21–40, 2009/1, available at: http://www.cairn.info/revue-psychotropes-2009-1-p-21.htm.
15 On collaborative work, the French Ministry of Industry already published in 2007 at the following address: http://www.industrie.gouv.fr/ sessi/4pages/239/index.htm; see also the work of Gérard Valenduc (2008); or (Carré, Lacroix, 2001). Also Luc Bonneville and Sylvie Grosjean (dir.), *Repenser la communication dans les organisations*, L'Harmattan, Paris, 2007.

media that is blatantly commercialized (McChesney, 2004, p. 138 and 143), notably under the influence of advertising and the cost-free digital economy.

The question of the economic exploitation of content and uses on the Internet, in particular, as well as on mobile devices (tablets and smartphones) with applications makes it urgent to work on social relations and expressions on very sophisticated platforms. The latter are apparently simple and easy to use as opposed to databases or to the forums of the 1980s and the 1990s, while it is now a data market. However, it is complex to work from economic determinism because of objectives of sharing and subjectivities from the users of these platforms. These are the subject of processing by the attention industries (Kessous, 2012; Citton, 2014) who point to customer loyalty, alertness and immersion, especially in video games[16], which are presented as models of invasive entertainment in serious or narrative form, matching the creation of consent (Chomsky, 2004, p. 33)[17]. We consider attention monitoring, which aims to retain even just for the time of the commercial or of the prescription of uses, or to immerse by interactivity and storytelling, and if immersion is seen as consent, in favor of those who have the power to control it, analysis can help to confirm the critical approach.

As a result, the formation of a digital culture is confirmed and digital uses are part of new cultural practices[18]. A technological culture has been refined beforehand thanks to computer experience, without allowing control of the publishing platforms, which capture the data in circulation.

16 See Dominique Boullier, "Les industries de l'attention : fidélisation, alerte ou immersion", *Réseaux*, vol. 2, no. 154, pp. 231–246, 2009.
17 Chomsky also quotes Walter Lippmann, *Public Opinion*, MacMillan Publishers, London, 1932.
18 Olivier Donnat, "Les pratiques culturelles des Français à l'ère numérique", 2008 survey, Ministry of Culture and Communication, 2008, available at: http://www.pratiquesculturelles.culture.gouv.fr/index.php.

While some amateurs bypass user manuals (or even standards of use), others, very enlightened, have the means to protect their data or even hide their activities online, with "onion" networks or, especially, the darknet (Gayard, 2017). However, these personalities, with their new distinction, are taken as examples in order to generalize the characteristics of the free and creative uses of DICT and digital networks at the beginning of the 21st Century. The appropriation for the general public concerns above all user-oriented functions, so that they can only operate what is finally authorized and interesting for the actors who make them available, within the framework of a cost-free market and the attractiveness of a "social web". During this time of strategy, the studies of uses, less and less registered in the sociology of uses – anchored in the 1990s – since uses are not an additional activity, but are at the heart of everyday life, accumulate to value the uses, caught in a process of intensive commercialization of human and social activities. The tactics are always confronted with the strategies and shed some light on them to stop the discourses and artifices and to demonstrate the inequalities of digital uses.

Digital precariousness illustrates the lure of discourses on democratization, when it is a question of mass dissemination and adoption of the uses of the Internet, from which it would be possible to see the ability of Internet users to articulate their uses of the Internet and their media practices in the context of entertainment in partially renewed forms by digital practices. Users with a strong cultural capital would still invest in the networks, consult cultural sites and participate in forums and digital social networks to establish new electronic sociability. It would be the same for the gender divide: various applications on the Internet are used mainly by men[19], who develop their IT culture, than women,

---

19 See the situation regarding gender in 2013: "L'internet de plus en plus prisé, l'internaute de plus en plus mobile", *INSEE Première*, no. 1452, June 2013, available at: https://www.insee.fr/fr/statistiques/1281312.

although women "have not been lagging behind" for more than 10 years[20].

Information technology is no longer the privilege of the professional and confidential uses of specialists. Computer tools are increasingly used for the industrialization of communication and culture, at a time of change in this field of research, especially within the creative industries[21]. These uses include not only cultural and communicational consumption and educational activities, but also activities such as recreation, advertising, fashion, gastronomy or tourism, to enhance the territories and their economic fabric, while soliciting the contribution measured by prescriptions of the users questioned by the discourses on their creativity. Thus, the Internet, transformed (partly) by economic actors into mass media with individualizing power, has become unavoidable in the context of these mutations, with ambivalent uses that reflect social and economic transformations. To take into account the rapid movements of networked digital technologies of a digital culture that is still diffuse and (will remain) unequal, it is advisable to put into perspective the process of qualitative studies of uses, in particular, the approach of appropriation. The latter must be systematically supplemented by socioeconomic data to contextualize the uses without extreme determinism. It is important to remember that the uses do not only concern consumer audiences, but also any individual in all circles and environments, supporting hyperconnectivity through digital technologies. The uses of these technologies are part

20 From the beginning of the 2000s: Claire Piau and Régis Bigot, Les opinions des femmes et des hommes sont-elles semblables ou différentes ?, Research paper no. 195, CREDOC, January 2004, available at: http://www. credoc.fr/pdf/Rech/C195.pdf.

21 *tic&société* journal, available at: http://ticetsociete.revues.org/747, see also the MSH Paris Nord seminar, available at: http://www.mshparisnord. org/actus/fichiers% 20pdf/industries_creatives_2008-2009.pdf.

of the ambivalence and the socioeconomic context of the digital industries.

3.2. Industrialization of the uses of interactivity: territories of hyperconnectivity

To analyze the intensive developments of the process of social computerization and uses of digital networks at the heart of discussed and permanent power relations, a policy of uninterrupted computerization witnessed for the last 50 years (Vitalis, 2016) must be considered. Now focused on the communication strategies of the digital and telecommunications industries, it brings in its wake the industries of culture and content.

Technological and societal dialectics operates by analyzing social issues and power relations in society in order to build a bridge between all the knowledge produced by the micro approach[22], with field studies leading to meso-level knowledge concerning practices and activity sectors, and commitment to macro-sociological questions.

Analyzing digital uses presents the opportunity to identify their place and role in the intensification of digital injunction, which is strategically renewed in order not to appear as such. Indeed, the strategy is to keep the user–consumers captive to permanent innovation, yet not allow most of them to have the time to master it, its foundations anchored in the spirit of capitalism that adapts and adjusts thanks precisely to perpetual changes, in spite of the corresponding tyrannies. Flexibility of the uses must resemble financial exchanges; besides, the value of digital relations is increasingly based on their measurement.

---

22 Approach to the sociology of DICT uses, which are less and less used to focus on operational approaches outside of social issues. The interactive and participative dimension now prevails to study the ergonomics and cognitive uses of communicating objects made commonplace.

Putting empirical work into perspective aims at engaging in a critical analysis of the notions of use and interactivity. It is no longer appropriate to isolate such notions in a single descriptive approach providing field data, since these refer to major concepts: emancipation and freedom. These notions also cover a fundamental constraint on individuals to confirm an economic system based on individualism that chants the horizontal distribution of powers, including the powers of creativity and entrepreneurship, so as to better manipulate and exploit the data engendered by hyperconnectivity. Interactivity, without naming it now – an expression abandoned and often replaced by "the user experience" – imposes itself as a matrix.

The debates held, especially until the early 2000s, on the notion of computer interactivity gave rise to three major types of definitions, ranging from the system of selection and manipulation of data to the interaction between human and machine and between humans, through the exchange of information between technological devices, controlled or not by human users. However, interactivity is also associated with monitoring and traceability, necessary for its development, and in terms of personalization and services, serving economic or social objectives. Indeed, on the networks, traced data make it possible to offer the connections, in a context of private interests based on proprietary logics, generating enclosures regarding the foundation of an Internet as digital common property (Massit- Folléa, 2012, pp. 153–178, Le Crosnier, 2015). In other words, it is for everyone and belonging to no one, while being a powerful carrier of standards. The emerging alternative dynamics of the digital commons[23] concern in particular the Internet, which appears as a "new common" presenting a "global community that collectively constructs

---

23 Hervé Le Crosnier, "Communs numériques et communs de la connaissance", *tic&société*, vol. 11, no. 2, 2017–2018 (forthcoming), available at: https://ticetsociete.revues.org/1966.

shareable and open resources" (Le Crosnier, 2015, p. 87). However, this digital common is confronted with enclosure strategies, with privatization and access limitation. Interestingly, these strategies are created with the same digital technologies as those with which the digital commons allow a movement favorable to the knowledge commons.

The enclosures are part of the informational and communication process based on computer interactivity, which presents diverse modalities: signs, messages, speech, writing, image, aesthetics, mediation, practice, experience, service, marketing strategy and social, economic, political and cultural innovations, in short, issues relating to power and freedom. These modalities evolve in a context of technical, economic and political sophistication of networks. These are masked by the discourses of companies, media and other engineers, about interactivity offering, allegedly, simplicity, intuitivity and freedom, in particular, to communicate. However, this liberating interactivity does not provide the opportunity to escape the captivity of data and the monitoring of social activities, or in other words, a reification of social relations. It is at this trouble spot that the question of interactivity, synonymous with diffusion and the facilitation of traceability, arises.

To further explore the notion of interactivity, it is important to remember that it is developed within different disciplines, first and foremost in the research in computer science and telecommunications that punctuates the technological evolutions captured by the engineers working with ergonomists referring to cognitive sciences, to work on the interfaces that reveal or mask the inscription of the use. Interactivity is also the subject of numerous studies providing specific insights into semiology, which offers the key of understanding the signs in constant evolution, such as the analysis of discourses on representations of interactivity, or aesthetics of new interactive experiences. The line of research on cultural industries provides the measure of an economy based, among other things, on these interactive technologies and on information diversity at a time of media concentration. The critical approach of the sociopolitics of uses highlights the political dimension of uses by articulating the technological, economic and social logics of the uses of digital technologies (Vitalis, 1994). The sociology of uses produces knowledge of the actual uses and of social appropriation of telecommunication, computer and editorial innovations, and on their insertion into pre-existing practices and their meanings. This multiplicity of studies confirms the need for an interdisciplinary approach to define interactivity, in order to continue the analysis of hyperconnectivity.

Concretely, interactivity, which implies a presence and a continuous participation of the user, is at the same time considered as favoring the symmetry of the exchanges and confused with the facility of diffusion of contents. The user is likely to become an issuer of information, with the electronic mail and digital social networks that constitute traceability and prescriptive devices, as part of a connection to different terminals, services, connected objects and other online platforms, including cloud computing. However, in these contexts of use, it should be remembered that emitters and receivers do not have the same equipment to access networks or to send and receive increasingly large multimedia documents. They have neither the same software knowledge to publish on the network or process data nor the same financial means to acquire digital production tools. Individual users tend to have much more limited means than companies and other institutions, and their goals are rarely economic strategies. We can however find expert users such as developers and other free-software enthusiasts or groups of individuals with well-defined objectives that can form experienced teams (such as certain collectives or NGOs capable of implementing lobbying actions via computer networks). Supporters of alternative licenses, such as the

Creative Commons licence initiated by Lawrence Lessig[24] and international networks, can also strategically organize their actions. To a lesser extent, groups around diversified interests are organizing themselves on the networks to carry out their activities and projects as they see fit.

For wider use, interactivity is also associated with the pleasure of choosing among the fragments, without being reduced to a tree view to be browsed in hyperchoice-based mode, with the customization of contents adapted according to labeled users (researchers, students, tourists, etc.) or according to online behavior, tracked in the context of Big Data. Nevertheless, the pleasure, in a content-sensitive relation and also with an interactive design, establishes relations to the digital objects coming from aesthetic of reception, as an experience, which is part of a horizon of expectation[25] based on previous experiences, in other words, a frame of reference in which cultural and communication practices interact. The development of personalized content, interactive interfaces and self-definition correspond to usage models built from trace or probability calculations from devices.

It should be remembered that a device fulfils a strategic function, networking what is said and what is hidden, and is therefore designed so that it adapts and adjusts the uses, in order to serve the initial interests, except in rare cases of bad buzz for example or of misappropriation, retaining that

---

24 See the following websites: http://fr.creativecommons.org/ and http://www.lessig.org/blog/.
25 Hans Robert Jauss addresses the literary work in *Pour une esthétique de la réception*, (*Toward an Aesthetic of Reception*) Paris, Gallimard, 1978. Yet, the concept of a horizon of expectation stemming from Jauss's aesthetic of reception theory must be kept in mind, which carries the entitlement to action of receivers and their anchoring in social norms in a world of shared references. Thus, the horizon of expectation is not a necessary framework, but is steeped in cultural references and sensitivities, which leads to break with the conception of an immediate experience, giving the aesthetic experience a cognitive function.

bypassing, confused with creativity, is more frequent and traced also to be integrated in industrial processes by marketing or commercial exploitation. Hence, the device embodies the domination of digital that led to its conception and realization. In an obscure and intrusive way, a collection of digital traces is processed from computing environments known as data warehouses, considerable data warehouses oriented toward decision-making and profiling, in spite of global respect of the French data privacy law[26], on the pretext of personalized services, although apparently fully provided.

Interactivity can thus become a constraint, or a paradoxical feeling of freedom, at the expense of traceability of behaviors and data, which became unavoidable, since Internet giants are even interested in the darknet (Gayard, 2017). This feeling of freedom can be connected to the place of the body[27], of the hand, almost always on the mouse or touch screen, which facilitate repetitions just by clicking or tapping on images, texts, menus or navigation bars and multimedia invitations from various applications. In addition, Internet users' publications are easily made with a few settings via interfaces that erase technical complexity. Without moving, using subterfuges within the technological devices, Internet users or players experience interactivity and the immediacy of access (to information, communication and publication methods) as a delectation, socially valued, to relive or invent sensations with meanings in their lives. The quest for immediacy during "transactions" made on or with digital applications can nevertheless be ergonomically disturbed. The user must then find the means to resume a download, update an application or even an operating system, query a database, seize apparently elusive objects, challenge the new codes of

---

26 Available at: https://www.cnil.fr/fr/loi-78-17-du-6-janvier-1978-modifiee; see also: https://www.cnil.fr/fr/textes-officiels-europeens-protection-donnees.
27 Geneviève Vidal, "Critique et plaisir au cœur des usages des médiations numériques muséale", *Interfaces Numériques*, vol. 3, no. 1, 2014.

interactive, non-intuitive user manuals as well as delete applications that consume the memory of the terminal.

If these constraints are rejected or criticized, then they sometimes engage users in a reflexive position. They then claim a conquest of technology, tactics implemented to avoid, circumvent, solve or take advantage of the problems that appear as such and are involved in the formation of a digital culture and of hyperconnectivity. This commitment to mediation, during which the body in front of the computer is one of its instruments, gives them the positive status of actors, that is, producers of meaning through their consultations and publications, who are previously registered in knowledge frameworks and cultural practices. The uses of interactive technologies are evidence of IT interactions, telecommunication and cultural practices. Users are integrated into processes of technological sophistication, aimed at mastering reception and digital consumption, participating in the renewal of the spectacle paradigm, which creates the social relations mediated by images, and via screens and dialogue boxes with multiple machines (Debord, 1992, p. 4). Within the scope of (tele)communication, the utopia of the power of the user, thanks to their participation in the mediation, indicates a will to differently appropriate online content and the modes of communication and publication, and to engage relationships with objects with no guarantee of a counterpower.

This synthesis of the characteristics of interactivity account for the matrix of interactivity opening on behaviors in front of the requirements integrated with the devices of the hyperconnectivity territories and in relation to the objects and data that make sense with the use, under surveillance by ingrained traceability and profiling techniques.

3.3. Uses of interactivity

The uses of interactivity seem to assist in the means of controlling the captivity situation on information and communication networks in accordance with contemporary social interactions, in a dialectical movement of limited alienation and disalienation of individual liberties (Lefebvre, 1961 p. 209). It is worth noting that control and social constraint are internalized by users[28]. Interactivity is indeed a widespread notion in society, including in social and commercial exchanges that systematically transform individuals into consumers aware of technical and economic determinisms.

The uses of interactivity lead to diversified objectives with sociotechnical and economic devices and configurations, which confuse freedom and domination. Current pervasive networks, such as the Internet of Things, distil intrusions up to the level of the users' bodies (equipped with mobile devices), caught in surrounding circuits that collect, without their knowledge, data useful for interpretations of communicating machines. In these conditions, how can the use of interactivity be interpreted as potential for inventions and creative rejections? Indeed, how can one reject or invent when the data are not voluntarily collected, but inserted in permanently connected terminals, where the digital invades all activities?

Interactive uses are no longer to be considered in an exteriority, but within the framework of appropriations that

---

28 The internalization of constraint and control by individuals has been particularly analyzed by Émile Durkheim (1975, pp. 22–31) and Pierre Bourdieu (1980, pp. 134–135).

give rise to interpretations through narratives[29], by composing with the contradictions, entanglements of narratives[30], "poaching" on the path from the self to the other. Subjectivities, without economic ambition, are thus exchanged, although these can be the subject of economic instrumentalization, in particular with publicity in search engines, spaces of publication or digital social networks. These expressions, increasingly characterized in terms of participation and contribution, would come from interactivity, often mistakenly confused with interaction (Proulx, Poissant and Sénécal, 2006), given the fact that interpersonal exchanges are realized through networks (via smartphones, computers and other terminals). Thus, the Internet and digital mobility networks would play a role in assertiveness and self-realization[31], in a process of awareness of the self and others, of political conscience developing the ability to identify data manipulations. These exchanges of subjectivities would not be limited to individualism, but would establish a knowledge of the self and make possible a

---

29 The narratives refer here to the work on time and long duration of Fernand Braudel. Reflecting on the long-term links between uses and narratives aims to establish a link between research on the uses of ICT and the relation to the world. The work of Fernand Braudel, *Civilisation matérielle, Economie et Capitalisme. XVᵉ–XVIIIᵉ siècle*, LGF/Livre de poche, Paris, 2000, in three volumes, just as Paul Ricœur's work on time and narrative (1983), contributes to a perspective of research on the uses of ICT.

30 M. de Certeau worked on the reading activity in particular, but Certeau is cited here for his analysis of narratives, which may lead to a fruitful reflection on the multiplicity of narratives on electronic networks (Certeau, 1990 p. 131).

31 The work of Michel Foucault (1984, pp. 53–85) on "self-cultivation", which has nothing to do with the Internet, can provide ideas for conceptualizing the uses of the Internet as "self-preoccupation", overlapping the issue of individualisation and singularities. Moreover, Foucault points out "the activity devoted to oneself ... not (as) an exercise of solitude, but (as) a real social practice", he reads "the work of oneself on oneself and the communication with others" (p. 67).

control of the interactive situation to act, in a potentially reflexive posture. Nothing is innovative in this human and social process, part of a social regularity without preventing infinite diversity[32].

After having determined the hyperconnectivity territories that rely on the uses of interactivity, in the context of the social appropriation of DICT that opens up a digital culture that prepares the minds for the exploitation of network connections, the reflection can go further with a renunciation of the traceability of data of all kinds generated by negotiated digital uses. In other words, this data monitoring, which in turn molds a digital culture, orients the acceptability of the omnipresent and permanent digital paradigm, but not without a negotiation of its uses.

---

32 This infiniteness is in the image of the dialectic individual/society, considering the communicating individual within the framework of a social regulation, source of fixity; see Simmel (1991). Indeed, the infinity that must be faced joins the impossibility of embracing the diversity of the world. Therefore, it is necessary to freeze and separate (Simmel's door metaphor) while connecting (Simmel's bridge metaphor). Dialectic linking/separating is, in certain ways, found on the Internet.

4

Renunciation and Negotiations

Digital uses prepare and maintain the social acceptability of hyperconnectivity data monitoring. This acceptability opens up to a renunciation that is inscribed in the heart of contemporary digital culture, which allows uses through negotiations. From this ambivalence of uses, in this chapter, we will explore the concept of negotiated renunciation (Vidal, 2010). To do this, it is first necessary to intensify the knowledge of the uses at the base of the renunciation and the negotiations of the users in touch with digital hyperconnectivity.

4.1. Uses at the foundation of renunciation and negotiations

The notion of use must be updated, given the need to update the frameworks to analyze digital technologies, particularly information and communication technologies, in their development conditions, not only from a technical perspective, but also from economic and political perspectives. As discussed, the social appropriation of digital technologies must be retained to analyze uses in economic environments based on the instrumentalization and the commercialization of traces and connection data on multiform networks. Social interactions, while being diversified, indicate conformity with the Internet network's standards of use, in particular, in its media and economic appropriation.

Would it not be illusory to consider the freedom of decision and expression through DICT, since the constraints are internalized and *a priori* limit freedoms, leading us to act in a determined manner? Users can, however, master (at least partially) the frameworks of these constraints, leading to the pleasure of the experience[1], which engages the emancipation of the "mind-numbing logic" of cause and effect since "emancipation opposes their dissociation" (Rancière, 2008, p. 20). Emancipation, with regard to the prescriptions and the execution of the plans designed by the designers and distributors of the technologies, makes it possible to abolish the distance[2] between *passive* reception (spectator) and *creative* action (actor)[3].

Identifying the uses is thus essential for a number of businesses and institutions, whether commercial or not, which carry usage studies[4] that refer most often to uses and ergonomics, more frequently to consultation statistics, to confirm their orientations in terms of digital strategy, in order to produce discourses linked to activity and the involvement of consumer-users. However, before considering active[5] users with interactive technologies, by exceeding

---

1 The typical case, encountered during the field studies, is the pleasure from the feeling of power of the users who think they have managed to overcome technical constraints or to simply have pleasure in the computer-mediated relation, from the content as well as from the communication modalities with interactive devices.

2 *Ibid.*, p. 10.

3 See also the conscience (particularly of determinisms) enabling action by Pierre Bourdieu (1994).

4 Some consulting firms and study centers: Ipsos MediaCT, Mediametrie, eStat, Nielsen NetRatings, GFK, Benchmark Group, NetValue, Sofres, CREDOC, as well as the DEP Ministry of Culture, university laboratories.

5 Active in the way the users would rely on a "creative capacity of communication and information" (Lefebvre, 1981, pp. 143–144).

functionalities, it is necessary to remember the fact that users rely on a social imagination, which gathers the individuals considered in a collective and individual autonomy, allowing DICT to be integrated in their daily lives, until they can no longer be detached, in short, in a voluntary non-disconnection.

Tracing the emergence of the notion of use is enlightening. It is with the functionalist current of uses and gratifications that the notion of use emerged in the 1960s. People want to know less about what the media does to individuals, and more about what media people do, which breaks with the effects paradigm. In the 1960s, reception studies began to develop, as well as cultural studies, for example, with a British research project from the Center for Contemporary Cultural Studies (CCCS) at the University of Birmingham. This work recognizes a form of receiver autonomy in relation to the media and their resisting capacity, while adopting a critical approach to the process of dominance for the majority of receivers. Even in the 1960s, diffusionism[6] regarded users as consumers who, following their interest, adopted innovations. They are classified into five categories: innovators, early adopters, early and late majorities and refractories. This model focused on describing the diffusion and circulation of innovations in society. The postulate, anchored in a technical and economic determinism, is centered on a rational consumer with freedom of choice. The diffusion theory offers a linear approach to technology diffusion, which is used to develop marketing strategies based on the growth phases of the technical innovation market. In the late 1960s, the sociology center of innovation, with the arrival of Bruno Latour in the early 1980s, focused on the negotiation process, the concessions between actors to design technical innovations (Akrich, 1993; Akrich, Callon and Latour, 2006; Latour and Woolgar, 1988). The concept of translation, which takes into account use in the design

---

6 Everett M. Rogers, *Diffusion of innovations*, Free Press, New York, 1962.

process, was thus elaborated when information and communication technologies based on computers and telecommunications were developing, an important phase when we think of a hyperconnected society. In the 1980s, in France, the sociology of uses emerged (Jouët, 2000, pp. 487–521), focusing "straightaway [...] on the technologies of information and communication"[7]. From the 1990s to the first decade of the 21st Century[8], this field analyzed social uses, the appropriation process of DICT (successively the computer, the videotex, the mobile phone and the Internet) and the dialogue between supply and evolution of uses (Perriault, 1989), without discrediting the weight of the offer before ruses and tactics (Certeau, 1990). The work deals with inventions, negotiations with prescriptions and meanings of uses. In a rejection of the technicist perspective, yet considering the uses as additional activity contrary to the current hyperconnected situation, several issues address social autonomy, the transformations of society, with the rise of individualism, while analyzing new forms of sociability.

Freedom of use thus constitutes a dominant ideology in society, but the economic appropriation of the Internet and digital media opens up to a media and commercial conception of uses. A certain control of the prescriptions of uses is then engaged by composing with opposition, in particular, to online advertising. As a result, companies are repositioning themselves to consider digital culture and appropriation that escape the radio-based media logic, and in the 2010s, strategies of prescription-masking emerged, valuing freedom, user power and creativity. However, the prescriptions are included in the paradigms relating to the uses of the DICT referring to activities, expressions and productions of individuals within the framework of a social

---

7 *Ibid.*, p. 491.
8 Serge Proulx (2001) proposes reconsidering the field of study of uses. Françoise Massit-Folléa (2002) draws up the "achievements and perspectives of research" in terms of ICT uses.

emancipation, in parallel with determinations. Thus, in a negotiated renunciation[9], the behaviors evolve according to an acceptance of the prescriptions in exchange for data and digital services. These negotiations are implemented through the same interactive technical devices that carry the objectives of diffusion and prescription (prescription by design) of the designers and suppliers. These negotiations are reflexive uses, which allow the users to act with omnipresent machines.

The analysis of the uses of digital devices makes it possible to identify new distribution methods and new prescriptions, including those from the users. These prescriptions indicate recommendations, as well as the relationship with data and content. This context of use sheds new light on innovations, in terms of prescriptions, in order to analyze digital practices and culture, of which both users and professionals are driven primarily by diffusion. A prescription regime of a new kind, beyond emission/reception, makes it possible to address the fact that interactive uses maintain prescription and contribute to the formation, maintenance or adoption of the prescription by algorithm. Instead of freeing themselves from it, users renounce and accept them via mediations and renewed forms

---

9 The notion of negotiated renunciation refers to the uses that are renounced by users with regard to their liberty to seize digital technologies and services and, at the same time, authors, by their resistance, of circumvention or even misappropriation thanks to their skills, experiences and critical posture, particularly via digital functionalities that make sense as they are used. The users do not regret this renunciation, which allows a pleasant position as issuers (of commands) and receivers (of content and services), such as the "opportunistic" users who can choose to download content without concern of coherence, to bring forward fragments of content, or others who can be characterized as "planners", who, on the contrary, try to see everything and achieve targeted objectives. Throughout their consultation, both types of users implement tactics to circumvent the problems encountered and to make their way through the reticular flows. See Vidal (2012).

of diffusion specific to hyperconnectivity. The latter take the form of a liberation inscribed in the paradigm of empowerment of individuals thanks to digital networks, within the framework of a certain lure organized by professionals to serve their interests. Thus, there is a multiplication of the prescriptions, thanks to Big Data and metadata contributing to the implementation of linked data, in the name of the adaptation of content in connection with the calculated consultations (except responsive design), as if the machines controlled the matching between supply and demand.

Work within the field of cultural industries emphasizes a conception of supply that structures uses, but media practices are not simply responses to impulses of supply. The critical posture that analyzes the relationships of power and domination within societies should certainly be retained from this field of research[10], because indeed there is no symmetrical relationship between designer and user. However, the works in this field of research are rarely linked with those on uses and resistances, or with the users' criticism, however limited, all the more in a context of technological sophistication, hyperconnectivity and inequalities of DICT access and uses. Combining work on the industrialization of culture and communication and that on uses is full of lessons on these said uses, recovered in the very conception of technologies. It is important not to overestimate the autonomy of individuals by their subject uses to economic logic and not to underestimate the role of structures. In other words, the dominant economic strategies in the fields of culture and communication are to be considered, without neglecting the empirical approach. This

10 The connivance of the field of cultural industries with the political economy of communication, which also gives great importance to the analysis of discourses, which aim to prepare the minds and to convince, makes it possible to link the economic and ideological dimensions of the discourses on culture, information and communication industries.

posture leads us to think dialectically of uses subject to economic logic, but at the same time of negotiations in the context of these logics.

In this second decade of the 21st Century, DICTs are socially accepted thanks to the belief in the "facilitation" of communication, production and access to information, and liberation from constraints, while at the same time creating new ones. However, it is important to go beyond the linear approach, which needs this situation to open up to representations dominated by social structures, in order to include it in a social diversity and in diverse subjectivities, so that the influence of individuals cannot be complete. However, digital environments, at all times and places, in society are imposed on individuals who accept and use them, often under pressure[11], in their personal and professional lives and in their social, professional and private activities. Yet, the coercive power of a normative society, which imposes norms, does not preclude the debating of digital technologies and the criticism of the injunctions of a digital economy and an invading equipped environment, claiming transparency instead of opacity.

Social computerization, which also concerns organizations, supports concrete relations with technologies that come mostly in the form of machines with interfaces of operation combination, participating in a technological culture and within a sociotechnological rationality. Technological performance is then part of a use of media and technologies that indicate to users the place they can, or even must, occupy as actors of a "digital society". The users thus increase their technical and ergonomic skills, which maintain their feeling of gaining power in the process of digital mediation. In an immediacy of the interactions between individuals and their environment, the norms of

11 Jacques Ellul (2004) clearly analyzes the situation of individuals "subject" to technical order.

which are incorporated as habitus (Bourdieu, 1980a, Bourdieu, 1980b, p. 134) and frameworks (Goffman, 1991), their experience infiltrates all activities. Thus, the digital skills are confirmed and enriched by composing a digital culture. The operating modes interweave with the representations of the devices deployed by users, a concept also to be questioned.

The transition from a concept of receptive audience to active users is concomitant to the development of the concept of interactivity, which marked the construction of a hyperconnected society. As mentioned, the receiver figure evolved in the 20th Century tracing a scale ranging from the receivers subject to the messages emitted, according to the limited effects theory (Katz, 2009, pp. 47–67), to the hyperactors considered amateurs[12], despite their much valued experience. The amateur is as much a user with multiple skills as the enthusiast with no specific skill, but a frequent consumer, like the Internet users visiting video platforms or those using peer-to-peer networks to download files, or even smartphone users, which have become ultra-light computers equipped with applications. The digital industries offer users mass customization based on a conception of interactivity as personalization. The user can then pick from the offer that makes all productions of the mind and of consumption accessible, building on reproducibility and dematerialization. The users are considered here as the ultimate unity of freedom, since they would be the pilots of the innovation, which would be realized by usage. The contribution of the sociology of innovation that developed the

---

12 See Antoine Hennion, "Ce que ne disent pas les chiffres... Vers une pragmatique du goût", in O. Donnat, P. Tolila (eds.), *Le(s) public(s) de la culture. Politiques publiques et équipements culturels*, Presses de Sciences Po, Paris, 2003, available at: http://www2.culture.gouv.fr/deps/colloque/hennion. pdf and http://halshs.archives-ouvertes.fr/.../Hennion2003Pragm PublicsDEP.pdf. Flichy Patrice, *Le sacre de l'amateur. Sociologie des passions ordinaires à l'ère numérique*, Le Seuil, Paris, 2010.

concept of inscription of uses, thought and stabilized by designers, of technical objects would be, according to this determinism, removed, insofar as the enlightened amateur is considered freed from all constraints thanks to interactivity. At the beginning of the 21st Century, the figure of the amateur tended to impose itself, since the user-amateurs have the power to test, experiment and influence, thanks to their force of reputation produced[13], on adjustments and developments, or even to provoke innovations in the context of rare horizontal uses (Hippel, 2007, pp. 293–315). According to this conception of the users' quality, the users have become able to manufacture (to become the makers) in fablabs and other "third places", such as co-working spaces, where they have become creative heroes and entrepreneurs ignoring intermediaries. Yet, what can be observed? Inequalities are omnipresent, and power and domination relations are very real.

From the evaluations inscribed in an updated functionalist idea of the limited impact of messages and influencers to those inscribed in a culturalist idea highlighting the capacity of users to select and decode the messages diffused according to their diversity and context, research has gone from the effects theory to a critical sociology of the media[14], via cultural studies and their survival by multiple declination. The users, with their power of opposition and negotiation in the relations with the issuer, adapt content through cultural interpretation (Mattelart and Neveu, 2003) despite unequal positions between users and issuers. As early as the 1990s, users have been thought of as

13 Given that amateur-expert users, thanks to their repeated uses, can arrogate the posture of the examiner, while demanding the right to be distracted, according to the term "distraction" by Walter Benjamin (2003).
14 Jensen Klaus Bruhn, Karl Erick Rosengren, "Cinq traditions à la recherche du public", *Hermès, la Revue*, nos 11–12, pp. 281–310, 1993.

individuals acting on content. They build meaning and become "co-authors" of sequences and associations of data online, thanks to their hypermediated paths that are increasingly traced. The empowerment of users thus joins the great story[15] of the end of the 20th Century. A majority of the current research on digital technologies also leans toward a design of a user-free concept of all experiences aiming at an auctorial function in content, which can act freely with software and applications, masking complexity thanks to recent intuitive interfaces. This user would then invent a collaborative and participative dynamic. This social recognition, reinforced by the dominant discourses, of the performance of the use of multiform computers connected to the Internet consolidates the feeling of action, echoing hyperconnectivity.

To define the user figure, it is also essential to work both on the channels of media and Internet use, and on everyday life habits,[16] bringing together group and affinity dynamics. Indeed, the extension of the meanings of distance communication and of information mediated with new information and communication devices based on interactive digital technologies tends to change the way the users think of themselves in a context of international networks. However, it

---

15 Philippe Quéau, founder of the Imagina festival of computer graphics in Monte Carlo and Director of the Information and IT Division of UNESCO between 1996 and 2003, published speeches on the Internet about the great story of the Internet. In regard to the term "great story", it can be noted that the online press, particularly Internet Actu, advocates the end of the great story and agrees with a complete social integration of freeing technologies, as this could be the end of a "computer and freedom" concept, and the rise of a self-regulation, since the users would have so much power (e.g. to self-defend their privacy).

16 This relies on the work on daily life of Certeau (1990) and Lefebvre (1961, 1981: pp. 143–144). See also André Vitalis, Jean-Claude Domenget, Karine Turcin, Temporalités médiatiques et vie quotidienne, Research Report, University of Bordeaux-3, 2004, available at: http://www.msha.fr/cemic/grem/axe1.htm.

must be remembered that users cannot be considered outside of a sociocultural context in which practices fit. Computer interactivity offered by online services nevertheless allows user interventions in the same way, since the participation framework provided by the issuers is identical on global platforms. Sometimes, participation is considered as alternative, even subversive (piracy, artistic creation), but institutions, destabilized, are led to deploy strategies adapted to these uses, so as to lead the vast majority to planned mediation. Some opposition will persist anyway. In both situations, access to digital networks gives the users the opportunity to assert a new form of distinction[17], based on their digital culture, which is currently being spread by the new touch screen devices that lead users to opt for readjustments specific to the paradigm of permanent technological innovation, at the heart of mainstream networks. Statistics show increasing Internet users and application users, through a policy supporting digital development in the second half of the 1990s, with digital public spaces and other places of public Internet and digital access, which were intended to transmit knowledge and skills in this area and played a discreet but effective role. Henceforth, the new public spaces, still necessary to support the growing digital culture, are called third places[18], joined by the less well-known living laboratory environments; libraries and other places of mediation engaged in digitization policies.

Access to digital experiences generally generates a virtuous circle to consolidate a powerful self-image, sometimes even supporting an entrepreneurial approach. However, this situation can also come with a feeling of frustration, either in terms of cultural ignorance or in terms

---

17 This refers to the work of sociologist Pierre Bourdieu on the concept of distinction. See Bourdieu (1979).
18 Benjamin Lorre, Les Tiers Lieux. Des métadispositifs issus de l'informatisation sociale, doctoral thesis in Information and Communication Sciences (LabSIC), University Paris-13 - USPC, 2017.

of technical limitations[19]. However, very popular games[20] and applications attract users thirsty for ergonomic comfort to enter playful scenarios encouraging action. The imagination relative to the potential of interactivity propagated by discourses, which are themselves propagators of utopias, pronounced or embodied in technical objects (Flichy, 2001), acts as a driving force to feel free to play, gather information, exchange more and enjoy, thanks to the digitization of all types of content and (potentially) to constant updates that punctuate the (equally constant) connection. A feeling of efficiency and of belonging to the great project of technological innovation is felt by the users, with interfaces that pretend to enable content and service manipulation at will. When websites are deemed experimental and original, such as artistic sites, Internet users, who do not give up despite the destabilization of their bearings and habits of use, also claim a position as explorers of new tracks on a reticular territory. However, being part of an unprecedented framework of use or even of illegal exchanges on peer-to-peer networks[21] does not always imply

---

19 This has been repeatedly observed, in particular, in different contexts of DICT uses: in exhibitions, net art sites and public connection places.

20 Not to mention console video games, online multiplayer games are massively used. The playfulness and creativity of Internet surfers can also be noted with fan-fiction on the Web. The theme of immersion seems to be crucial for actors working on games.

21 Clandestine encrypted networks went through the first wave of regulation with Dadvsi, then Hadopi; see Geneviève Vidal, "Online debate and transposition of the European Copyright Directive into French law", *International Journal of Electronic Governance*, vol. 1, no. 2, pp. 231–239, 2008, available at: http://www.metapress.com/content/q22n7512q836/?p=e16753b439a640b184a0a8f630305504&pi=0. See also Geneviève Vidal, Caroline Angé, "Les usages de l'internet : de la fragmentation au rassemblement", *EUTIC 2006 Enjeux et usages des TIC. Reliance sociale et insertion professionnelle*, Brussels, Belgium, 13–15 September 2006. To extend the analysis of the uses of interactivity, militant actions mediated and implemented via the Internet have been explored, see Geneviève Vidal, Vincent Mabillott, "Compétences sur l'internet : adaptation, résistance des utilisateurs de P2P et mobilisation des internautes pour intervenir dans le débat public", *EUTIC 2007 Enjeux et Usages des*

being a hyperactor, especially when audiovisual culture steps in during consultations, when the interpretation of a proposal leads to being immersed without functional intervention. Thus, Internet users seek a position of reading, visualization and enjoyment, while claiming they want a consultation in sound and image, without being in moments of passivity. Each user may be different depending on his/her mood or availability. It is thus possible to adopt an interactive approach at one moment and to not want to intervene at another, engaging the reconciliation between critical attitude and enjoyment of the show or content flow (Benjamin, 2003).

When users adopt a critical attitude, they demonstrate that they are not subjugated by technology, even if they claim to be destabilized, astonished or if they claim power with interactivity, which can become a constraint, in a paradoxical feeling of freedom of use. In fact, to overcome the constraint, while mixing in the pleasure of interactivity, users, driven by the representation of digital networks as a "territory" of possibilities, experience emotions, while drawing from the memory of their past emotions, during their cultural practices (exhibitions, cinema, video games, literature, etc.). The appropriation of digital technologies indeed leads to interactions of computing, telecommunication and audiovisual and cultural practices[22], which open up to manipulations of hypermediatized content, ideally offering multiple pathways to draw personalized paths and

---

Technologies de l'Information et de la Communication, Athens, Greece, 7–10 November 2007; Olivier Blondeau, "P2P, vidéos, Mediascape", *Médiamorphoses*, no. 21, pp. 49–53, 2007.
22 Geneviève Vidal, L'appropriation sociale du multimédia de musée. Les interactions entre pratiques de musée et de multimédia de musée, thesis, University Paris-8, 1999.

readings[23]. In doing so, the posture regarding computers refers to industrial cultural consumer products.

As a result, users are composing and entering into a slow process of transformation of access to digital services and content, in order to find or invent meaningful experiences in their lives. The utopia of user power, thanks to their participation in mediation, indicates a will to appropriate online content differently without making possible the will of appropriating the means of production by the users as it is operated by issuers[24]. They express themselves on digital social networks – to keep in touch with the network of "friends"[25], "fans" or members of professional "communities", which would otherwise be lost – or on institutional websites providing moderation of user interventions, which form new relationships with content, including participatory and contributory situations. The screen thus presents itself as an interface of a variety of content, cultural, educational, commercial, entertaining, administrative or professional, and of a participative fervor. Also called Web 2.0, this participatory Web has revived the Internet's economy over the last 12 years, yet it does not prevent a distribution of inequalities in terms of publication. Indeed, being mainly receivers of multimedia objects, Internet users follow an online movement, with a minority engaged in publication and another even more restricted minority, which develops, in an impulse (that seems altruistic), the software or online

23 See, for example, the work of Brigitte Juanals on online reading: "Encyclopédies en ligne : un modèle du lecteur électronique", *Hermès, la Revue,* no. 39, 2004.

24 This observation is persistent, but the discourses keep repeating that amateurs or at least "pro-ams" now have the same tools as the experts they can compete with. For Internet users who do not claim a pro-am stance, but who benefit from discourses promoting their power, it can be observed that it was mostly only a possibility and an intention to send an e-mail or express themselves on the networks.

25 Facebook "friends" are either "accepted" or "ignored", reducing friendship, a fundamental human value, to a "I take, I leave".

spaces enabling the circulation of non-institutional content on the network. However, all these expressions are the object of an industrialization of communication. Nevertheless, actions on a network such as the Internet are part of a great tradition of human reciprocity, with its obligations and duties, including donations[26] sometimes, considering that a donation also faces a standardization process, which comes with recovery or adaptation of online inventions. Internet users thus participate in the maintenance of the media system, which supports the capitalist system and social relations. Users, who invest their time and skills in the purchase of hardware, software and telecommunications, talk to each other on the Internet (Tisseron, 2001) with seemingly nothing to hide[27], in a (remarkably) transparent society.

From the concepts of users, uses and interactivity, it should be remembered that these have marked an epistemological turning point, in the way of considering research on media and DICT, even in the way of considering social sciences, which seize information and communicational objects in society. Information and communication sciences occupy a preponderant place in the framework of this dynamic of hyperconnectivity analysis, and go beyond functions and effects, in reference to a thesis by Wright Mills (2006) as early as 1959. By inscribing this analysis in a critical perspective, this work will opt for empirical studies of uses, which go beyond satisfaction to reach the ambivalences and meanings of use, following a sociopolitical posture opening up to the concept of negotiated renunciation.

---

26 Alain Caillé, *Anthropologie du don*, La Découverte, Paris, 2007.

27 "Extimacy" on social networks, coming from an expressive individualism, see for example: Allard Laurence, "Express yourself 2.0!", in Eric Maigret, Eric Macé, *Penser les médiacultures*, pp. 145–172, Armand Colin/INA, Paris, 2005.

4.2. Negotiated renunciation

This commitment, between empirical and conceptual approaches for a critical posture, supports the analysis of uses, being the object of a renunciation by users of some of their freedoms in order to seize technologies and digital services with which they negotiate. They are indeed authors, through their resistance, bypassing, or even misappropriation, using digital features, via their skills and experiences, and deploying a critical posture thanks to the meanings of uses. Negotiated renunciation thus also takes into account the prescription of interactive technologies disseminated in society and the misconduct[28] of users (most often) aware of their renunciation in the domestic sphere, at work, during their communicational, cultural and mobility practice.

The freedom to act in a hyperconnected society should thus not be denied, even if technologies are increasingly at the service of the economy on the lookout for their uses. Hence, the concept of negotiated renunciation makes it possible to grasp the ambivalence of digital uses and proves to be relevant when considering the dialectics of the compliance of user-subjects with the technical system[29] and social appropriation.

This concept also helps to put the notions of use and interactivity into perspective. It is often about power without discussion from the moment when users seize technologies, as actors of digital devices. Thus, far from being linear and tidy, the appropriation process of interactive and

---

28 This capacity refers to the idea of an active reception of cultural content as has been developed within the British cultural studies line of research; work relying on the questioning of the notions of culture and power relating to the reception of the media and the cultural industries. See Mattelart and Neveu (1996).
29 Technical system characterized in particular by rationality, autonomy, artificiality, growth and universalism (Ellul, 1990).

interconnected technologies is changing. In other words, the situations of use multiply and renew themselves, interweave, differ from or elude more or less to the designers' logic, making it impossible to predict all the uses of technological devices[30]. This complex dynamic probably explains why users encountered during the field studies feel like they negotiate[31] with the designers thanks to their devices, caught in a "chaotic process" due to negotiations, in terms of resistance and opposition, or even protest, with established conventions and to limit their monitoring.

"Negotiated renunciation", resulting from a work to conceptualize more than 10 years of field studies, simultaneously takes into account the injunction of digital technologies disseminated in society and user misconduct, aware of their submission[32] to DICT in the domestic sphere,

---

30 As far as professional situations are concerned, studies of computer-supported cooperative work (CSCW) also seem interesting to identify the gaps between design and uses (Robinson, 1995).

31 See, in particular, a 2004 study (Geneviève Vidal, Emmanuel Paris, Etude des usages du Minisat et de Visite+, report submitted to the French Department of Public Studies, City of Science and Industry), during which the users explicitly expressed the feeling of renunciation with an augmented reality device. This feeling was thus the subject of an analysis in terms of negotiation (a term not explicitly pronounced) with this renunciation felt, given the attempts to make the device work according to their objectives of consultation (up to temporarily ignoring the device). The device is, in this context of exhibition visit ("Canada really" at the City of Sciences and Industry), "experienced" as a production of the museum, whom they trust and de facto the users rely on the institution for guidance and support. It is also obvious here how much the context of uses in a museum is rich in information about negotiated uses of interactivity.

32 This consciousness of submission to the injunction, of the partial alienation of its own uses, is the foundation of tyranny, since this renunciation (which is more than obedience, as La Boétie (1530–1563) exposes it in his "discourse of voluntary servitude") aims at a negotiation, for and by the self, to be part or even to participate in the network of "support for tyranny", in an interdependence of unequal power relations. The users are in fact accomplices of the cultural system, which alienates them (La Boétie, 1995).

at work and in mobility. This concept takes into consideration two forces that seem to oppose each other: to be acted on and to be an actor. Indeed, empowerment through digital and reticular technologies updates the issue of prescription, understood as imposing knowledge and skills on individuals, which would allow them to empower themselves. This prescription is intimately linked to mediation policies, since it involves giving standardized answers to individual requests. The prescription is of a deeply contractual nature, inasmuch as the individual must agree to give up some of his/her liberties if he/she wants to acquire new ones. When this renunciation is repeated enough times, especially in the context of technical processes, relations of domination are established between technical systems, driven by the economic sphere and now increasingly by the administrative sphere with digital teleservices, and individual users, or even associations or collectives. This case is a prescription translated within informational, communicational and transactional devices, which are part of the hyperconnection context. However, the terms of the exchange are not always adapted to each situation of use experienced and they sometimes lead to misunderstandings. By being lost, unable to be understood, to express what is experienced, to correct the human/machine dialog, users decide to lose some elements gathered during their consultations; for example, they might give up not only the possibility of consulting all the content but also the way the designers had planned its uses. This renunciation is not necessarily regretted by the users, who consider it as a means of freeing themselves from the numerous social constraints and as a decision allowing for a better position in connection with the feeling of "being able to do everything".

To consider this dialectic, we must remember the industrialization of culture, communication and social interactions, while referring, as is proposed here, to the sociology of everyday life[33]. As early as 1981, Henri Lefebvre[34] identified the issues of power and domination in everyday life with the arrival of "technological innovations"[35]. However, several questions must also be addressed, especially the strategies of economic actors seeking to structure the uses, without concern for the wealth of appropriation (Massit-Folléa, 2002). Appropriation, discussed in Chapter 3, is a complex process to analyze, requiring both quantitative and qualitative approaches, which cannot be reduced to access or to the characterization of user-consumers and their uses, as tiny as they may be. Uses are formed through permanent adjustments in everyday life, at the very heart of domination relations. These adjustments, evidence of user negotiations, are the result of economic, political and individual actors, sometimes even grouped together[36]. They all have specific goals and powers.

---

33 It should be noted that daily life can be considered as a minor or major research object, between an underestimation that does not make it possible to grasp the structuring issues of the reproduction of the domination relations and an overestimation of the subjects' resistance in their daily lives.

34 In Volume 2 of his *Critique de la vie quotidienne* (1961, p. 28), Henri Lefebvre asks the question of the critique of everyday life in philosophy or in social sciences.

35 Henri Lefebvre devoted a sub-chapter on "informational and everyday life" (pp. 135–153), at the end of the book before the conclusion. IT and telematics are mentioned on page 135.

36 Gilles Pronovost (1994) thus states the difficulty of "separating what concerns, on the one hand, the capacities of cultural innovations, of the deviations from the situation, of decentration and of the capacity of action that must be recognized by the actors, and, on the other hand, the anteriority and the domination of the industrial offer". See Gilles Pronovost, "Médias : éléments pour l'étude de la formation des usages sociaux", *TIS*, vol. 6, no. 4, 1994, p. 378, online: http://revues. mshparisnord.org/disparues/index.php?id=870.

To further the exploration of negotiated renunciation, which seeks to define modalities, by renunciation, of the recording of the negotiations of users/actors of the traceability of hyperconnected data, the terms composing it should first be defined.

The term "negotiated" refers to the work on cultural industries and cultural studies, which will be cross-analyzed here. The first field of research marks social uses as belonging to "a social dialectic, a negotiated construct"[37]. Indeed, "at the beginning and throughout the process of implementation and generalization of a technology, we are dealing with uses and not with real social uses[38]. These uses should only be considered as 'contributions' to the formation process of uses"[39]. Here, "negotiated" refers to a "dialectical adjustment process between mass production and consumption"[40].

The term "negotiated" can also be linked to the work on the active reception of cultural content, as has been developed within current British cultural studies research, mentioned previously. From questioning the culture and power related to the reception of the media and productions of the cultural industries, Stuart Hall (1994, pp. 27–39) has deployed an analysis model based on the notions of "coding" and "decoding" and, in particular,

---

37 Jean-Guy Lacroix, Bernard Miège, Pierre Moeglin, Patrick Pajon, Gaëtan Tremblay, "La convergence des télécommunications et de l'audiovisuel : un renouvellement de perspective s'impose", *TIS*, vol. 5, no. 1, pp. 81–105, 1992, available at: http://revues.mshparisnord.org/lodel/disparues/docannexe/file/103/TIS_vol5_n1_4_p81_105.pdf.

38 The endnote contained in this excerpt defines "social uses" as "modes of use that manifest themselves with enough recurrence, in the form of habits sufficiently integrated into everyday life, to fit in and impose themselves in the range of pre-existing cultural practices, to reproduce and possibly resist as specific practices" (*Ibid.*, p. 101).

39 *Ibid.*

40 *Ibid.*, p. 95.

"negotiated decoding", a blend of opposition and adaptation. The receiver partially modifies the meanings of the message. He/she accepts the message conveyed, but adapts it or opposes it in a limited way. Stuart Hall notes that dominant decoding is the most common and considers that power is omnipresent. However, mass culture is not considered as directly alienating. Indeed, negotiation stems from a critical posture[41], intersecting work in the political economy of communication, which questions the processes of production and distribution, the reproduction modalities of the domination structure (Garnham, 2006).

This dialectical and critical posture toward negotiated uses of digital technologies is also mobilized through renunciation, which marks unequal power relations between users and manufacturers (IT and telecommunications, on the one hand, and cultural content producers, on the other), without denying the uses in terms of negotiations, as we conceptualize them based on years of field studies. Following the example of Mattelart and Neveu (1996), attention should be paid to the criticism of ethnographic works inscribed (especially after the first founding movement of cultural studies[42]) in a movement focused on

---

41 In the context of political economy, a critique of the design of a power of resistance, emancipation from oppression and domination by the receivers, can be pursued within cultural studies (Kellner, 1997, p. 103), as Stuart Hall was able to support by working on the meanings of mediatized content.

42 Cultural studies have paved the way for a large number of studies from around the world such as those on gender, postcolonialism, the struggles of ethnic and homosexual minorities and rehabilitation of mass culture (comic books, television programs, novels) and rejection of the elitist positions of literary or cinematographic studies. In this expansive version, we retain the excesses of work that underestimate social and economic determinisms. Cultural studies tend to put the importance of the strategies of information and cultural production companies into perspective.

active subjects and free to select following self-assessed needs. However, we know all the flexibility and scope of the user's "freedom" and their great ability to decode cultural products, while the relations to culture remain unequal. Richard Hoggart has worked on the influence of the media on popular culture while denouncing the tendency to overestimate it and remaining wary of the tendency to industrialize culture[43]. As a result, he considers, in particular, the working-class alienated by mass media, but by working on popular press, he notices that his reading is not the subject of a passive reception; that it shows circumvention, inventions and resistance. Thus, Hoggart[44] speaks of a working class culture, which seeks to distance itself from living and working conditions. He notes the importance of the household, of the neighborhood, which plays a role in the reception of media in everyday life. In a post-Marxist perspective, culturalist researchers believe that history rests on social struggles that have since been transformed and that it is important to work on everyday practices of resistance to the capitalist system, embodied here by the technologies of hyperconnectivity. The work thus simultaneously addresses media practices and practices in everyday life, taking into account social and cultural contexts. However, it should be noted that there are limits to research that takes the point of view of the user-actor in order to study the construction of the relation between the user and the media. The social and cultural origins of the

---

43 Cultural studies, however, stand out from the current of research on cultural industries, by Max Horkheimer and Theodor W. Adorno, 1974, pp. 129–176.
44 Richard Hoggart, who is working class and a professor of literature in Britain, published *The Uses of Literacy* in 1957 (Richard Hoggart, *La culture du pauvre*, Éditions de Minuit, Paris, 1970).

founding researchers of cultural studies[45] can explain this axiological choice to suppose that the individual can live singular experiences outside of all determinisms. It is true that their work seems to promote popular culture. Nevertheless, the originality of this current of research remains marked by work centered on ordinary lifestyles and cultural identities. When cultural studies focus on working on negotiated decoding in reception, they refer to the power of opposition and adaptation of the users able to determine the meanings of the messages.

More recently, the work on Internet use has highlighted negotiations as being the traces of individuals' activity, who communicate on electronic networks (Barats, 2013; Cardon, 2008, pp. 93–137). This indicates the meaning given to the term "negotiated" in cultural studies, namely the challenge of encoded meaning or even personal and collective meanings. With regard to digital uses, technical skills (from ergonomic and cognitive points of view) support negotiation, in terms of interactivity between functionalities (those made available by the provider) and reference frameworks for the user, who seize the same technologies to publish, manufacture and broadcast on the digital industry's platforms. This work's analyses make it possible to put into perspective the power of users of digital technology, yet without removing it. This is why negotiation can be articulated with renunciation.

---

45 Richard Hoggart with Edward P. Thompson and Raymond Williams founded Cultural Studies, the confluence of literature, anthropology and sociology. Raymond Williams, also working class, and Edward P. Thompson, historian, wanted to go beyond the purely economic analyses of culture. Stuart Hall, Jamaican-born, settled in the United Kingdom "bearing" British colonization.

Renunciation refers to the subjection to market forces, which creates and organizes constraints, inequalities and satisfactions for its subsistence. The uses are thus at the heart of appealing marketing techniques. These techniques must make the users accept the processing of personal data and connections or downloads for the establishment of personalized services or the provision of publication spaces in which even the criticism of these strategies is possible. Renunciation thus takes place when the users let the companies (media, search engines, access providers, online services, advertisers, etc.) track their activities and their content, to obtain, in return, in a negotiated way, Internet services (digital social networks, publishing software, e-mail clients, search tools, information and resource sites) or other local networks. To a certain extent, the users give up some of their freedoms and rights to obtain others, more exactly presented as such. Freedom, at the heart of renunciation, would be housed in services (free and payable) offered on a market of information, communication and social interaction. However, the user's freedom cannot be limited to negotiation with the technologies and the content, derived or vectorized by the industry.

Étienne de La Boétie's "speech of voluntary servitude", to further the reflection on the term "renunciation", shows a great entanglement between uses and power. According to La Boétie, there would be servitude, consent and tyranny, either out of habit or by a chain of interests to submit to tyranny to be part of the network and thus make tyranny "enslave subjects one by another" (La Boétie, 1995, p. 40). Power would therefore be permanent and everywhere to maintain "voluntary servitude".

Renunciation can still refer to "consent"[46]. However, renouncing does not require (consent under) threat, as there would be conditions. The term "consent" would include accepting under conditions, under duress, yet it is the nodal point with renunciation, which refers to constraint without preventing the sometimes inventive, bypasses, of those who renounce.

To define the term "renunciation", it must also be remembered that renunciation occurs when, on the one hand, there is awareness, or at least understanding, of the partial and continuous alienation by the user and, on the other hand, when there is, at least to a certain extent, critical will and resistance to this condition. Indeed, when there is discernment of determinisms and prescriptions, there is a possibility of action. It can also be considered that the experience of use can break with a "low level of technology" and de facto with "technological alienation" (Lefebvre, 1961, p. 211). Would it mean considering that uses with much less skill are more subject to renunciation and partial alienation? When there is, moreover, a certain critical will toward the forms of alienation, renunciation can intervene as circumvention and action, by a series of negotiations. Nevertheless, can renunciation be considered when there is agreement by compromise with technology? Indeed, renunciation cannot be thought in such contexts of use[47].

---

46 The term "consent" refers to the work of Maurice Godelier, whose anthropological approach might further this analysis. However, it is important to keep in mind that the work of Maurice Godelier deals, in particular, with male–female domination relations (Baruya) and that consent is part of specific violent relations. Maurice Godelier, *La production des Grands hommes. Pouvoir et domination masculine chez les Baruya de Nouvelle-Guinée*, Fayard, Paris, 1982.

47 The question of non-renunciation can indeed be asked, since users, who are nevertheless capable of discerning power relations in the context of ICT uses, may not be able to apprehend them in a renunciation, for example, having to give personal data, which can be processed in marketable databases, or knowing that the uses are traced to obtain an

However, compromise is somehow like negotiation and we can thus go back to renunciation as long as there is negotiation. What seems tautological here, while bearing in mind that negotiation evolves on renunciation's territory, meets the dialectical stance necessary to analyze the complexity of renunciation, much less studied than that of negotiation.

Exploration to define both the terms "renunciation" and "negotiated" leads to this concept as a contribution to articulately analyze the processes of industrialization and commodification of culture, information and communication and practices of daily life, in which digital information and communication technologies are intensively integrated, joining the framework of hyperconnectivity. Indeed, everyday life, as a place of transformation and continuity (Lefebvre, 1981, p. 49)[48], is crossed by what Henri Lefebvre calls "technological modernism" (Lefebvre, 1981, p. 52). In fact, the question of uses in a double dimension, micro and mesosociological (uses, practices and representations of technical objects) and macrosociological (cultural matrices and sociopolitical contexts)[49], must be considered in this dialectic.

After having developed a reflection on the economic issues (Chapters 1 and 2) and then social issues (Chapters 3 and 4) of hyperconnectivity, this work will now continue by studying environmental issues. However, before that, it seems useful to very briefly review the results of the analysis

---

online service. They should not consider negotiations; would they not simply be in a state of consumption of a service? But even if we maintain the question, these users are not always and only in this situation.

48 It can also be noted in this respect: "The humble event of daily life appears to me then in two aspects: a small individual and accidental fact - a social fact infinitely complex and richer than the multiple 'essence' it contains and wraps. The social phenomenon is defined by the unity of these two aspects" (Lefebvre, 1945–47/1958, p. 67).

49 From Massit-Folléa, 2002, p. 5.

conducted so far. The creation of an industrial offer accompanied by diversified services has contributed to a globalization of connection and to the diffusion of content by communication industrialists. The diffusion of uses on a planetary scale and their proliferation cannot be understood without taking into account three main characteristics: (1) a mode of access and use proposing free services to the users of these sociotechnical devices; (2) a method of indirect financing relying on two specificities, the sale of advertising spaces and the valorization and marketing of personal data and (3) a mode of activation, the unbridled, if not productivist, solicitation of all, industrialists, communities and users. This socioeconomic model, described as a model of "hyperconnectivity", results in unprecedented data production, display and circulation that also favors unparalleled social surveillance and control. In the configuration studied, the State accompanies and stimulates the digital economy. Only the necessary injunction of hyperconnectivity enables the longevity of the socioeconomic model, favoring a hyperconnective use of the connection, which in turn leaves more traces of personal data. As the freedom to act, publish, exchange and express oneself extends, the social control extends as well by feeding on the technical traces, the content left by the Internet users by connecting, while navigating, and the assiduity consented to appear, to reveal themselves voluntarily. Given the importance of these devices in relational, communicational or sociability practices, it is important to understand the main social and environmental (i.e. ecological) issues. It is not about addressing and listing all the social and environmental issues, but about focusing only on those of importance related to this hyperconnectivity, from its "rematerialization".

5

Environmental Issues

Since 2 August 2017, humanity has been living beyond its means. In other words, after 8 months and 2 days, the inhabitants of our planet consume what the Earth can produce in 1 year. At present, it would take the equivalent of 1.7 Earths to meet the current world consumption. At this rate, two planets would be needed in 2030. If every inhabitant adopted the way of life of a North American, it would take four planets today, given the ecological footprint of the United States[1]. It is a growth model that has been questioned several times since the 1970s[2] and remains reluctant towards sobriety since it is pushing for

---

1 And yet on 1 June 2017, President Trump announced that the United States was withdrawing from the Paris Agreement, stating that it was too unfavorable to his country's economy. In his speech, he indicated that this withdrawal would allow him to save many jobs in the coal industry.

2 1972: Club of Rome, report on the limits of growth and depletion of resources; 1987: United Nations World Commission for Environment and Development, Brundtland report that defines the principle of sustainability as development that meets the current needs without compromising future generations; 1998: Kyoto Protocol – International treaty to reduce emissions of gases that cause global warming through the greenhouse effect; 2015: COP 21 – Paris Agreement on climate, the first universal climate agreement to try to limit the rise of temperature to 2°C. It follows negotiations held at the Paris Conference of the United Nations Framework Convention on climate change.

overproduction and overconsumption, with severe consequences on biodiversity and climate change. The relational opulence implemented by the DICT, contrary to what is too often asserted, participates fully in it, and hence it must, for the reasons that have just been briefly mentioned above, be also understood in its environmental dimension. It must be remembered that even if the discursive productions put forward the expressions "virtual world", "cloud computing" (what a bucolic metaphor!), "data lakes" (data sharing between non-competing companies), "data farming" and "server farms", this very productive connection is actually based on material goods as it shall be seen.

Therefore, after having examined the economic and social issues of hyperconnectivity, it is neither understandable nor tenable, at the beginning of the 21st Century, to not examine these issues taking into account the environmental (ecological) issues. In its fifth report published in 2014, the IPCC – Intergovernmental Panel on Climate Change – shows that climate change has already started and has just been confirmed once again by the COP 23 held in Bonn in autumn 2017. This change is at the same time one of the greatest challenges for humanity and one of the most important signs of our overconsumption, even if the climate skeptics resist and persevere. Their arguments include various positions, as Olivier Godard (2012, pp. 46–69) showed very well, ranging from nuclear defense, through the manipulation of the United Nations, to the attempt of applied science to monopolize the budgets of fundamental research. However, it is also a way to denounce IPCC's fundamentalism, the return of millenarianism or a strategy to favor the lobbies of the oil and automobile industry. We remember that in 2017, the environmental dimension was far from being integrated in the studies conducted on digital development, with too few exceptions, even if there have been encouraging developments in the last few years. At the time of global warming disruption caused by human activities and the exhaustion, or even the finiteness of resources, this dimension should be systematically considered and become unavoidable.

The Earth has certainly known, in its long history, important climatic evolutions, but they were over the course of a very long time, spanning tens or hundreds of thousands of years or even more. The climatic evolution generated by human production, especially the industrialization of activities, goes back a few hundred years and has provoked, according to climate experts, changes on an excessively short time frame, within a human lifetime. First, the development of fossil fuels (coal, gas, oil, etc.) has been significant since the 18th Century and then the industrial, agricultural and mobility processes produce increasing amount of greenhouse gases (GHGs), the main contributor of which is carbon dioxide (CO_2). The concentration of CO_2 has been rapidly increasing in the atmosphere (>40% in two centuries), thereby causing global warming and major disruptions: melting of the ice caps, glaciers, rising sea and ocean levels, not to mention their acidification, more intense weather variations, loss of biodiversity and so on.

5.1. Absence of environmental dimension

Unrestrained digital, relational and communicational practices have an impact on the environmental issue, and although lamented upon in 2012[3], through an examination of the French scientific literature in this field, even if it is possible to see some evolutions, the environmental issue is

---

3 Dominique Carré, "Approche critique des techniques numériques d'info-communication : Vers la prise en compte d'une nouvelle dimension ?", *80ᵉ Congrès de l'ACFAS : Où (en) est la critique en communication ?*, Montréal, Canada, 1st–11th May 2012, available at: http://www.cricis.uqam.ca/IMG/pdf/ActesColloqueOu-_en_-est-la-critique-en-communication_Gricis2012_Reduit.pdf.

absent or remains very withdrawn from the economic, social or legal dimensions, with some exceptions, such as the work by Fabrice Flipo, Michelle Dobré and Marion Michot, *La face cachée du numérique. L'impact environnemental des nouvelles technologies* or the articles by Hervé Le Crosnier *"De l'immatériel énergivore à l'énergie sociale des réseaux de communication"* or Fabrice Flipo and Cédric Gossart *"Infrastructure numérique et environnement"*. According to official reports, they are almost non-existent except for the one commissioned in 2008 by the French Ministry of Ecology, Energy, Sustainable Development and Spatial Planning and the French Ministry of Economy, Industry and Employment, the objective of which was to assess the environmental impacts of information and communication technologies (ICT) and their contribution to the fight against climate change (Breuil, Burette, Flüry-Hérard, Cueugniet and Vignolles, 2008). To a certain extent, it is also possible to retain the green paper published by Syntec in 2011.

In fact, the environmental issue emerged later in France (1960s–1970s) than in other European countries and for many years there was no difference in France between economic growth and environmental protection, even if a very few studies, conducted as early as in the period 1950s–1960s, began to question this relationship[4]. The proliferation of climate skeptics and the indifference of the vast majority can also be pointed out.

It may be admitted that many contributions prior to the 2000s do not include the environmental dimension of the

---

4 Particularly, the work of Bertrand de Jouvenel: *La Terre est petite* (1959), *Introduction au problème de l'Arcadie* (1965), *Pour une conscience écologique* (1965), *Les économistes et l'environnement* (1971–1972). It is possible to refer to these texts in a publication that gathers a set of texts by Bertrand de Jouvenel, *Arcadie. Essais sur le mieux-vivre*, Gallimard, Paris, 2002.

DICT in the analysis techniques developed, but it seems inconceivable that this situation will persist in the future, given the importance of environmental issues in contemporary society. As an illustration, there are two publications, among others, from recognized authors, with very important publications in the French-speaking academic world: one deals with the industrialization of information and communication and the other one with uses. In the first one, by Bernard Miège, published in 2007, *La société conquise par la communication. Les TIC entre innovation technique et ancrage social*, not a single line is dedicated to the environmental issue. The other, published by Francis Jauréguiberry and Serge Proulx in 2011, reviews the uses and challenges of communication technologies (*Les Usages et enjeux des technologies de communication*) over a 30-year period, and the environmental dimension is also absent. Only the work of Ivan Illich, one of the most critical authors on the misdeeds of industrial society and technologies, is referenced. These authors[5] rightly indicated that Illich excludes communication technologies from his criticism, claiming they are "liberating", "friendly" and not "polluting". The others are described as dangerous and alienating. This absence is also noteworthy in more specialized publications, as evidenced by a white paper published in November 2011 on open data and the stakes and opportunities for the company (*Open data: quelles enjeux et opportunités pour l'entreprise*). It was carried out[6] in partnership with some large French companies (SNCF, La Poste Group, Suez environnement, etc.). It discusses data opening, the impact on businesses and the success factors, but the environmental challenges of open data are not even addressed. Fortunately, sites like GreenIT, Novethic take into account the social and environmental dimensions of DICT and inform about the effects of digital technologies on the environment.

---

5 Francis Jaurréguiberry and Serge Proulx.
6 On an initiative by the Bluenove research company.

Nevertheless, Illich's viewpoint sheds light, in a way, on the Francophone situation. The DICTs are too often perceived as non-polluting, with the ability to replace or solve transport and traveling problems that create pollution. These technologies are then perceived as tools in the service of the environment, not to say of the ecological transition, and for the most enthusiastic, they might even be able to solve the "environmental crisis", or at least be an indispensable tool to implement the oxymoron sustainable development. This is the case, among others, of the work of Sylvie Faucheux, Christelle Hue and Isabelle Nicolai, *Tic et développement durable. Les conditions du succès*[7], or the journal *Terminal*, which has published several texts, especially in 2011, in issue number 106-107: *Le développement durable à l'épreuve des TIC*. ICTs are thus considered "green" technologies promoting sustainable development. Yet, as early as 1998, Gérard Valenduc and Patricia Vendramin questioned the true ecological dimension of teleworking. The assessment made is far from obvious, and the authors specify that the real assets of this mode of organization should be sought somewhere other than in energy savings and that it is important to consider the "rebound effect", also called the Jevons paradox[8], which can be stated as follows: the more the technological improvements increase the efficiency with which a resource is used, the more the total consumption of this resource will tend to increase, instead of decreasing. Thus, the more dematerialization is developed, the more the number of products and services consuming resources and energy increases and therefore the predicted environmental impact is much weakened. The main conclusion of the authors is that "the environmental argument must be used with extreme caution when it comes to promoting teleworking" (Valenduc and Vendramin, 1988, p. 86).

---

7 Published in 2010 by Boeck editions, Brussels.
8 Named after William Stanley Jevons, British economist.

Let us say then that, these technologies are seen as convivial. Their conviviality would favor the connection of individuals, durability of exchanges and increase of social links in an increasingly individualizing society. Their conviviality would also, according to Illich's reasoning, exempt DICTs from any aspect of negativity. On studying social criticism in the field of information technology and society, a change of mind can be observed, not to say a reversal of perspectives (Carré, 2005, pp. 91–100). In the late 1970s, social criticism focused on the limits of computerization, the negative repercussions of technology, the deterioration of working conditions and the fears they place on individual and collective freedoms. Criticism has shifted since the 2000s, and it no longer consists of questioning the limits of social computerization, as for the question of the finality of the technique, it seems evanescent. Most actors are calling for faster computerization and universal access to the Internet in order to reduce the "digital gap". It went from questioning the limits of computerization to a social criticism that aims to appeal to the "democratization" of the Internet, to free access to promote the use of this technology by the greatest number, demanding increasing number of technologies, more infrastructures and even more uses, to such an extent that a certain convergence between critical discourses and promotional speeches can be seen. Trade productivity would then save society, but perhaps not save the planet?

We can also say that, they are seen as liberating. In this case, DICTs are presented as an unmatched means of expression, mobilization, resistance to strengthen the democratic functioning of societies and challenging the powers in place. As indicated by André Vitalis (2016), new technologies do not only serve the dominant powers, but they can also be made to serve causes. In this context, DICTs are part of a social emancipation process that allows active minorities to intervene in the public space. Perceived as liberating and with democratic virtues, these technologies are highly valued. The more Internet exchanges, the more publications on digital social networks, blogs, sites, as well as online petitions, the better the democracy would be. Why not? Is this not certain? It is, however, certain that the unbridled increase in relational exchanges has consequences on the energy consumption and *de facto* on the production of carbon dioxide (CO_2) and greenhouse gases (GHGs).

Thus, the relational and communicational opulence favored by DICTs must be grasped, in the current context of global warming, in its material dimension (equipment) and also in terms of usage (proliferation and diversification of uses). Even the truly immaterial part (software, avatars) must be rematerialized. Frequented by millions of users worldwide, Second Life illustrates the rise of virtual universes that require energy-intensive servers. Nicholas Carr, an American journalist, tried in 2007 to evaluate the energy footprint of an "inhabitant" of this online world. It turned out that a virtual "avatar" consumed annually about 1,752 kWh, as much energy as a "real Brazilian"[9].

5.2. Materiality of the immaterial

Undeniably, the digital world enjoys a "clean", "non-polluting" image, which undoubtedly results from the way of naming the technologies that compose it and the social representations associated with it: circulating electrons, dematerialization, virtualization, instant and trace-free duplicability and software immateriality, even if the use of software, as will be seen later, has very material consequences. Barbara Duden[10] stated that for Illich, we

---

9 Available at: http://www.novethic.fr/empreinte-terre/economie-circulaire/isr-rse/un-avatar-virtuel-consomme-autant-d-energie-qu-un-vrai-bresilien-1083 65.html, consulted on 21 September 2017.
10 Barbara Duden, "Illich, seconde période", *Esprit*, p. 156, August–September 2010.

must be liberated not so much from the technologies and institutions, but from the representations and modes of perception they generate. It is therefore necessary to adopt a process of materialization or, more precisely, rematerialization of the intangible in order to better understand the environmental issues that arise from hyperconnectivity.

The following six main characteristics stand out from the ICT and sustainable development report (*TIC et Développement durable*) published in December 2008 at the request of two French ministries:

1) The electricity consumption of ICTs is increasing and is currently at 58.5 TWh per year, or 13.5% of France's electricity consumption.

2) ICTs (including audiovisual products) in the residential sector represent 30% of a household's electricity consumption (excluding heating, domestic hot water and cooking), which was only 10% in 1995. We note that the "standby" of equipment (including ADSL boxes) alone constitutes 10% of household electricity consumption.

3) The overall increase in consumption by households on white household appliances (cold, washing and lighting) was offset by the increase in household ICT equipment and their high electricity consumption levels.

4) The overall carbon footprint of ICTs is estimated at 30.18 Mt CO_2/year, or 5% of GHGs – with a margin of error of 30% according to ADEME – that is, more than aviation worldwide (2%)[11]. It should be noted that the carbon footprint of equipment production is greater than that of their uses[12]. The reason for this is likely to be found in the

11 Impact undervalued and disputed by many experts.
12 ADEME estimates that 1 euro spent on computer equipment generates 900 g of CO_2.

highly nuclear nature of the electricity produced in France. If the commonly accepted figures when the share of electricity does not come from nuclear power were used, then the electricity consumption of DICTs would generate a much higher carbon footprint. France is therefore an atypical case.

5) The electricity consumption increases by 10% per year. Despite the industrialists' efforts to develop less-energy-intensive equipment, technological developments leave little hope for reversing the situation in the future.

6) The use of ICTs reduces CO_2 emissions from other industries as the positive impact of these technologies on the whole economy would make the ICT sector reduce its own greenhouse gas emissions one to four times. This seems far from obvious in 2017 with the consideration, as seen before, of the "rebound effect".

To better understand the need to rematerialize the immaterial, two examples are provided by the French Environment and Energy Management Agency (ADEME) to illustrate and appreciate what is being played out from technical, energetic and environmental viewpoints when establishing a productive relationship and a daily hyperconnectivity of uses. Two publications were selected from this agency to assess the multitude of exchanges, the necessarily industrial nature of the activity that is deployed on the Internet and the production of greenhouse gases. The first one is the little ADEME guide published in October 2011: *Les TIC, quels impacts?*. Analysis of the lifecycle of Information and Communication Technologies (ICTs) shows that they have much impact in terms of energy and raw material consumption and pollutant emissions, often hazardous waste and GHG.

Moreover, it shows that the electricity consumption of ICTs is steadily increasing by 10% per year. This increase results especially from ADSL (Asymmetric Digital Subscriber Line) connection boxes usually working around the clock. As for paper consumption and travel, they do not seem to be decreasing.

Two main indicators reflect, according to ADEME, the impact on the environment of the use of ICTs: the "climatic" impact associated with the energy consumption linked to the production and use of materials and the "potential metal depletion", which reflects the use of rare metals in the electronics industry. This can be illustrated by two practical cases, because there are very few Internet users who are aware of the real environmental impact of sending emails and browsing the Web. Regarding the climate impact of emails, it was assessed, considering the French context[13], that sending 33 emails of 1 Mb to two recipients per day per person generates annual emissions equivalent to 180 kg of CO_2, that is, more than 1,000 km traveled by a car. Multiplying the number of email recipients by 10 would quadruple its climate impact. The impact of raw material consumption is also significant. Sending an email with a 1 Mb attachment consumes the equivalent of 7.5 g of iron, the weight of a 1 euro coin. Decreasing the impression rate of emails received by companies of 100 people by 10% would, according to ADEME, yield a gain of 5 tons of CO_2 equivalent over 1 year. This is the equivalent of about five Paris–New York round trips.

As for Web requests, directly going to a website by entering the address or registering it as a favorite instead of using a search engine reduces GHG emissions fourfold. The

13 We remember that the primary energy in electricity is mostly produced by nuclear plants with low CO_2 emissions, even if they have other very significant risks, whether on short or very long term. If electricity was produced by coal or gas plants, then the impact would be much higher.

advantage is even greater for the impact of "raw material consumption", which goes from 5.5 g to 0.3 equivalents of iron if we consult five search results to find information or if we directly go to a website's address. It is also worth remembering that a laptop consumes 50–80% less energy than a desktop computer.

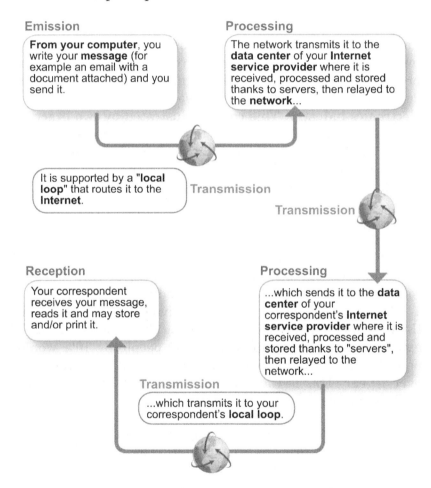

Emission

From your computer, you write your message (for example an email with a document attached) and you send it.

It is supported by a "local loop" that routes it to the Internet.

Transmission

Processing

The network transmits it to the data center of your Internet service provider where it is received, processed and stored thanks to servers, then relayed to the network...

Transmission

Reception

Your correspondent receives your message, reads it and may store and/or print it.

Transmission

...which transmits it to your correspondent's local loop.

Processing

...which sends it to the data center of your correspondent's Internet service provider where it is received, processed and stored thanks to "servers", then relayed to the network...

Figure 5.1. *What happens when we send an email? (source: ADEME, 2011)*

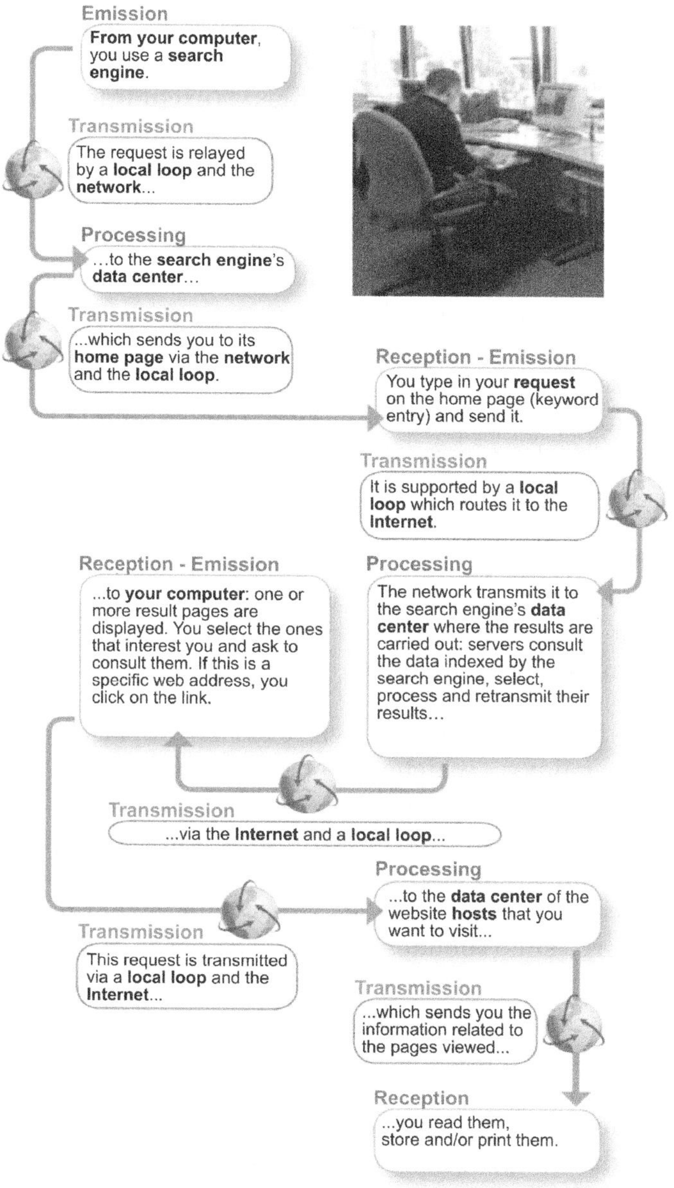

Emission

From your computer, you use a **search engine**.

Transmission

The request is relayed by a **local loop** and the **network**...

Processing

...to the **search engine's data center**...

Transmission

...which sends you to its **home page** via the **network** and the **local loop**.

Reception - Emission

You type in your **request** on the home page (keyword entry) and send it.

Transmission

It is supported by a **local loop** which routes it to the **Internet**.

Reception - Emission

...to **your computer**: one or more result pages are displayed. You select the ones that interest you and ask to consult them. If this is a specific web address, you click on the link.

Processing

The network transmits it to the search engine's **data center** where the results are carried out: servers consult the data indexed by the search engine, select, process and retransmit their results...

Transmission

...via the **Internet** and a **local loop**...

Processing

...to the **data center** of the website **hosts** that you want to visit...

Transmission

This request is transmitted via a **local loop** and the **Internet**...

Transmission

...which sends you the information related to the pages viewed...

Reception

...you read them, store and/or print them.

Figure 5.2. *What happens during a Web request? (source: ADEME, 2011)*

The second, very recent, publication dates from the spring of 2017 and informs about the very real, material aspect of the digital galaxy. ADEME estimates that every hour 1.6 billion emails are exchanged (excluding spam) and 180 million requests are made via the Google search engine alone, and to serve all users worldwide, 45 billion servers are required. This is obviously a strong industrialization of exchanges that continues to grow. As for the distance traveled by digital data, it would be approximately 15,000 km (email, download, request, etc.), and as for the greenhouse gas emissions by the digital galaxy, they are distributed as follows: 25% come from data centers, 28% from infrastructure and 47% from equipment owned by users. Cloud computing requires almost permanent connections and a constant back and forth between users, sites, socio-digital networks and platforms. It is important to note that carrying data on the Internet consumes twice as much energy as storing it locally for a year. Real digital factories and data centers are home to thousands of energy-intensive computers.

As it has just been shown with two specific cases, the Internet galaxy, which is often forgotten, is above all composed of a vast energy-intensive technical infrastructure on a planetary scale containing a multitude of IT and telecommunication equipment used both during the emission and reception of an electronic message for example (computers, smartphones, tablets, Internet routers, storage disks, printers, scanners) when transmitting this message (copper, optical fiber or satellites networks, submarine cables, various electrical and electronic equipment, switches, repeaters, routers) or when processing data (data servers, application servers, robots to browse the Web, storage arrays, data centers, air conditioners, cooling systems). Not to mention, of course, the software and buildings that host all these facilities. The reader will agree that all this is not immaterial or virtual but quite the contrary – even if some servers can be – and require resources to produce and maintain daily operations. Materiality is too often overlooked, but it is at the heart of any digital device. As for the frequency of access, the multitude of uses and the frenzy of exchanges, all this contributes to generating a significant global environmental impact on a daily basis. We remember that in 2017 it was estimated that more than 3.5 billion people were connected to the Internet. As for international data flows, they would have been, according to experts, multiplied by 45 since 2005 to reach 400,000 gigabits per second.

By following the steps of the lifecycle analysis (LCA) of a product, a study that makes an exhaustive inventory of all the components used in the manufacture of a product and the energy and material expenses throughout its lifecycle, it is possible to highlight the following four main steps:

1) extraction of raw materials, metals and rare-earth elements;

2) production of hardware, software and their marketing;

3) use of DICT;

4) landfilling or recycling.

Without denying the importance of metal mining[14] and rare earth excavations that generate pools of toxic sludge, they also cause depletion of soils and groundwater, leading to the loss of biodiversity while affecting the health of workers and inhabitants. The analysis conducted here on

---

14 Ferrous (steel), non-ferrous (copper, aluminum), precious metals (gold, silver), strategic metals (tantalum, lithium) and rare-earth elements (lanthanides), whose extraction is extremely polluting and which are used in the manufacture of batteries, LEDs, cell phones, microcomputers, computer screens and so on.

hyperconnectivity will not take into account this environmental dimension.

Issues related to the end of life of equipment (landfilling, recycling) that pose many environmental and health problems will also be dropped. Taking them into better consideration could delay, in the current context of knowledge, scarcity and depletion of scarce or non-renewable resources.

Similarly, this work will not directly engage in the production of materials and their marketing, which are very energy-intensive, in order to focus on three important dimensions, often little investigated and in direct connection with an economy of hyperconnectivity, contributing to the increase of the carbon footprint (CO_2) and to the greenhouse effect, which are sources of climate change.

First, the importance of energy consumption and the impact this hyperconnectivity can have on GHG production are taken into account. The second step is the analysis of the software design process, which has consequences on their use, energy consumption and the production of GHG. Finally, in the third and final step, the role of planned, injunctive and ecological obsolescence is observed.

5.3. Energy consumption and greenhouse gas production

If equipment production, as seen earlier, constitutes the most important part of electricity consumption, then the electricity consumed during the daily operation of equipment, networks and servers significantly contributes to the increase of energy consumption and GHG production, a source of global warming. Evaluating the impact of hyperconnectivity, not only in France, but globally, is not easy and remains poorly documented or dependent too often on partial analyses, but the hypothesis formulated here, based on observations and investigations, is that the share of energy consumption related to the use of DICTs is increasing and will undeniably, in the future, become more important. Five factors are to be considered. The first is the multiplication and the increasingly massive diffusion of these technologies among businesses and individuals. The second results from the importance gained by communicational opulence, the evolution of the modes of sociability and the intensive use of DICTs, henceforth part of all social practices, whether professional, friendly, recreational, administrative or cultural. The third takes into account the deployment of mobile Internet (4G and future 5G) to address the increasing importance of the bandwidth required for online videos and connected objects[15]. The fourth is less known and stems from the importance of online advertising which is very energy-intensive. The fifth and final factor results from the extension of the use of DICTs in geographical areas that are only recently affected or which are only affected on a small scale for the moment and where the production of electricity is primarily from a fossil fuel source and therefore a carbon energy.

---

15 Telecommunications operators offering very high speed, 4G, connections in a situation of mobility greatly favor "data" traffic. Studies have shown that, compared to an identical bandwidth Wi-Fi connection, data exchange consumes 15 times more energy in 3G and 23 times more energy in 4G than in Wi-Fi. 4G has undeniably favored digital uses since the use made by the majority of individuals is to connect to digital social networks and to watch videos. Operators have understood this very well since they offer increasingly unlimited packages. 4G is not yet deployed in all territories, 5G is announced to increase the transmission speed (300 Mbits/s for 4G to 10 Gbits/s for 5G), but its specificity is not based on speed, but on the reduction of latency in the transmission of data in order to optimize the reaction time to meet new uses: connected objects, autonomous cars, augmented reality.

What is interesting here, obviously, is not the strict energy consumption, necessary to make the Internet work and the technical configurations that result from it, but also the origin and the nature of electricity production. Does it come from a non-renewable fossil source (coal, gas, oil, uranium)? Or from renewable carbon-free energy (sun, wind, water)? Thus the way electricity is produced is not without consequence on the environmental impact and in particular the tonnage of carbon dioxide (CO_2) and methane (CH_4) produced, sources of the greenhouse effect.

Since France differs from most countries in the world by producing electricity in nuclear power plants, it is also interesting to evaluate the tonnage of radioactive waste produced each year. The website GreenIT.fr tried in a partial way to shed some light on this. The three largest French websites total approximately 30 billion page views per year, which generates about 1 ton of radioactive waste. This is of little importance from a quantitative viewpoint, but it must be remembered that radioactive waste, even in infinitesimal quantities, is extremely hazardous.

Greenpeace's "Coal in the Cloud" campaign results from the "How Clean is Your Cloud?" report[16]. This publication examines the cloud services produced by data centers. As a result, the demand for electricity generated[17] by this activity increases exponentially, but the main conclusion is that it is mostly satisfied by carbon-energy sources, such as coal, which are dangerous to health and have a significant impact on greenhouse gas production. Despite progress being made to limit digital energy consumption, efforts have not led so far to any real energy savings because of the significant growth in cloud computing practices. A report published in

16 How Clean is Your Cloud?, Report, Greenpeace International, p. 3, April 2012.
17 Some data centres consume the equivalent of about 250,000 European households.

2013 by Mark P. Mills from the Digital Power Group indicates that *The Cloud Begins With Coal* and estimates that the entire digital ecosystem accounts for 10% of the electricity produced in the world[18] or 50% more than the global aerospace business. The report points to three important elements. The first is that despite their growth, data centers would only represent 20% of the electricity consumed by digital devices and networks. The electric power of data centers in 2012 worldwide corresponds to the production capacity of 30 nuclear power plants (Glanz, 2012). The second is that charging a smartphone or a tablet requires only a negligible amount of electricity; however, watching one hour of videos per week consumes more electricity per year than two refrigerators over a year. What about the 500 billion emails exchanged every day in the world[19]?

The third is that the demand for use of data centers will increase faster than their gains in energy efficiency, so the amount of electricity will continue to increase significantly and will be produced with coal. We remember that, at present, the world's electricity production is mainly based on coal (46%) and gas (23%). According to the International Energy Agency, coal-fired power plants would have provided 68% of the increase in electricity capacity worldwide despite the development of renewable energies (RE).

It is important to identify the source of electricity, since many new data centers are located in areas where electricity is produced from coal or diesel (petroleum). This is the case in India. The cloud has become one of the drivers of diesel

---

18 This represents the annual consumption of Germany and Japan combined. Note that some experts believe that this figure is more significant: between 13 and 15%.
19 According to ADEME in 2013.

demand needed to power generators. It is a very polluting source of energy, just like coal, because it contributes to the significant amount of CO_2 and GHG emission, which also contributes to the diffusion of particulates (PM 10, PM 5) causing health damage. However, this is also the case in the United States, where, in order to produce cheap electricity, the Internet industrialists have reactivated coal plants, especially in the Appalachians. It is important to note that operating data centers also requires a significant amount of energy to run the cooling systems for computer equipment. New processes are certainly being experimented with or progressively implemented, such as water cooling or free cooling processes, which involves using non-energy-consuming methods to cool the equipment, such as the supply of fresh outdoor air or cold water or even recovering heat to supply urban heating networks.

As we can see, the impact of DICTs on the climate has recently attracted research attention. It is now necessary to consolidate certain results, to develop study fields, to set up more efficient[20] methodologies or to consider new areas of investigation. It seems that it would be relevant to analyze, for example, the way in which the communication industry is putting data centers located in the world in competition with each other in order to obtain the quickest response to a request. There is no doubt that this type of request has a significant impact on GHG production during each request.

---

20 As the Bio Intelligence Service did on behalf of ADEME: comparative analysis of the environmental impacts of electronic communication, summary, July 2011. In this study, we find reference scenarios to establish specific results, for example, sending a 1 Mb email to a person; sending a 1 Mb email to several people; sending a 1 Mb email to a person who will print the attachment and management of the email box. This approach has been extended not only to Web requests but also to the USB key.

The major communication industrial groups (Apple, Google, etc.) increasingly invest in renewable energies to power their equipment by using photovoltaic panels, geothermal or wind power and hydraulics or water or air to decrease the temperature of data centers. We recall that in 2012 Greenpeace published the list of the 14 Net giants[21]. It showed that while some groups (Yahoo, Dell) get more than 50% of their power from renewable energy, the others still relied heavily on coal (Apple, 55.1%; HP, 49.7%; IBM, 49.5%; Oracle, 48.7%; Microsoft, 39.3%; Facebook, 39.4%). On the contrary, some hosts, such as Infomaniak, power their data centers and offices with 80% of energy from hydropower and 20% from other renewable energy sources while giving priority, in most cases, to air control techniques without cold production, and in the winter, the heat released by the equipment is recycled to heat the premises.

The investments of the Net giants should amplify, in the coming years, renewable energies in order to develop their activities for two reasons. First, it allows them to reinforce their brand image by communicating about the creation of data centers that use renewable energies. Second, lawyers are starting to look into the induced liability for investments made on global warming. Assuming that it is difficult to convince billions of people not to use carbon energy, 350.org and Divest Invest have deferred responsibility to a few major energy and GHG producers, especially the 20 largest industrial companies[22] in the sector, which produce 29.34% of the total CO_2 and CH_4 (methane) emissions. The aim is to encourage the institutions that manage collective savings (banks, insurance and pension funds among others) to withdraw their investments from public or private

---

21 *How Clean is Your Cloud?*, report, Greenpeace, April 2012.
22 Examples include Chevron (USA), ExxonMobil (USA), Saudi Aramco (Saudi Arabia), BP (Great Britain), Gazprom (Russia), Pemex (Mexico), Coal (India), Total (France), National Iranian Oil (Iran), Royal Dutch Shell (the Netherlands) and Petroleos de Venezuela.

companies involved in fossil fuel extraction in order to keep it in the ground. Apparently, this action is starting to bear fruit, since at the end of 2015, more than 3,400 billion dollars had already been disinvested, even though this may not be enough. It should be considered that at every stage, extraction, exploitation, export and consumption, the fossil energy industry enjoys immense tax benefits and favors from governments. The International Monetary Fund (IMF) has calculated that globally, every minute the fossil fuel sector receives, as noted by David Coady, Ian Parry, Louis Sears and Baoping Shang (2015), €9 million subsidies in cash or in kind.

Officially, in France, GHG emissions are decreasing, but it is without taking into account that it buys increasing amounts of goods or services that are no longer produced on national territory, but imported, and those CO_2 emissions are not counted because they are not generated at the place of consumption. This is the case, for example, for most DICTs. ADEME indicates that from 1990 to 2007 if emissions from France dropped by 7%, emissions from its inhabitants increased by 14% and reached 8.8 tons of CO_2 equivalent per person. The resulting emissions of imports would thus represent 44% of the emissions of French households in 2007.

While some major Internet and online service providers are investing in renewable energies, as was just discussed, the global development of the cloud is leading to an increasing use of fossil fuels, thus increasing CO_2 and GHG emission, a source of global warming. It must be noted that 69% of the energy produced still comes from coal and gas and that the global investment in renewable energies (hydroelectric, wind or solar power) decreased by 18% in 2016. This situation results from the exploitation, particularly in the United States and in Canada, as well as in other countries, of shale gas and bituminous oil with deplorable extraction methods that can destroy landscapes and biodiversity, pollute groundwater and even produce mini-earthquakes.

It must be remembered that according to Illich, the abundance of energy leads to exploitation more than the thirst for fuel. For social relations to be equitable, society itself should limit the energy consumption of its most powerful citizens. Thus, only a policy of low energy consumption would allow, according to this author, a variety of lifestyles and cultures (Illich, 1975). In the early 21st Century, it was necessary to revise the formula and replace it by the abundance of CO_2, which leads to the exploitation and destruction of the planet. Only a policy of low production and carbon consumption would allow a variety of lifestyles and cultures. In other words, is an excess of technical and energetic means necessary to fully experience the relationships required for our professional, family or social lives?

5.4. Impacts of software and website design

Software has become, first and foremost, a service that can be accessed online or downloaded from the cloud, which is itself hosted in data centers. The white paper published by KaliTerre, EasyVirt and A2JV with the support of ADEME[23] indicates that reducing the needs of the software layer would reduce the need for computer equipment and power and cooling systems. The power consumption of data centers would automatically decrease as a whole. This cascading effect would have an impact on the exploitation phase,

---

23 The study focused on the energy consumption of computer equipment used in the professional world. It is based on 50 audits conducted in Pays de la Loire, Brittany and Poitou-Charentes between 2012 and 2015.

not only on the electricity consumption, but also on the investment to be made, since too often server rooms become oversized. It should be noted that this impact would affect all the characteristics of the infrastructure, starting with the power expected from inverters, transformers, air-conditioning and so on. Thus, 1 W power saved at the server level would save a total of 2.8 W from the cumulated gains[24].

The work carried out by Françoise Berthoud, a research engineer in computer science and Director of the ÉconInfo group at the CNRS, shows that the evolution of the material has created a "limitless" culture among developers. The following is the conclusion she draws:

> "There was a time when the quality of a code was measured by its performance compared to the resources used. It was the time when the processor capabilities, the amount of RAM or the storage capacity were real limits that were taken into account [...] A time when we recognized a good developer by their ability to fit their code in the small allocated area. These things were precious. That was ten years ago [...] there is (today) a craze for software development where efficiency is measured in working time for the computer engineer and not in efficiency compared to resources. And never mind if this precipitation translates into ever more energy-intensive software since the resources are perceived as "virtual" and therefore "unlimited": when it "lags", just replace your Smartphone or tablet with a more powerful model and there you go. Anyway, the code will be obsolete by the next

24 Source Emerson 2007, cited by KaliTerre, EasyVirt and A2JV, in the white paper published in October 2015.

generation of equipment and it will have to be rewritten. The consequences are not visible at the timescale of software development: why worry about other things?" (Berthoud, 2015, p. 5, foreword by Bordage)

The criticism addressed to developers is that they program as quickly as possible without taking into account architecture or software optimization in order to release a new version before competitors. And what about the trend to offer increasing number of features, which most users will ignore they exist? These directions result in the "bloatwares", which require greater resources in terms of not only processors but also RAM, not to mention disk space thus forcing the users to buy more powerful equipment to use this software.

Frédéric Bordage (2015), developer, software architect, co-founder of the GreenIT.fr Alliance and author of a book on Web eco-design, agrees with Françoise Berthoud's comments and shows that the ecological footprint of websites has been consistently increasing over the last few years. The reason is that they are poorly designed, as evidenced, still according to this author, by the weight of Web pages, which increased six times between 2008 and 2015. We could consider that it improved the definition and quality of Web pages. It is not so. This practice, according to Bordage, is inherent in the current site design and penalizes the user since the pages are slower to load, which affects energy consumption and global warming. As another example, it is preferable during the interface development to use "assisted input" rather than "autocomplete"[25]. Indeed, although autocompletion is very user-friendly, it has a major drawback: it requires

---

25 "Autocomplete" refers to a computer feature that allows the users to limit the amount of information they enter with their keyboard, by being offered a complement that may be suitable for the string of characters they started to enter.

substantial back and forth between the browser and the servers on the networks in terms of requests and leads to higher electricity consumption, resulting in greenhouse gas production. Conversely, assisted input guides the user through a set of information and clues, displays error messages, helps detect incorrect entries and, moreover, without making the use heavier, avoids incessant back and forth between the user and the server. On a large scale, the energy savings are significant and reduce the ecological footprint.

The environmental footprint of the Web is difficult to evaluate because some data are missing. Despite this, it is possible, according to Bordage (2015, pp. 18–20)[26], to give in a generic way, that is, without it being possible to isolate the use, an order of magnitude. Considering the life span of infrastructures and equipment and their use, the global annual Web footprint would be at least 1037 TWh of electricity, or 40–50 nuclear power plants, which is twice the electricity consumption of France, that is, 608 million tons equivalent of greenhouse gases and 8.8 billion m^3 of water. If the number of Internet users on the planet is estimated to be 3 billion, then the annual footprint per user would be approximately 342 kWh of electricity, 203 kg of greenhouse gases and 3,000 l of water consumed.

It is important to note that the production of electricity consumed by Internet users, the network, data centers or access centers for applications and their cooling mainly worsen the impacts. In France, where electricity is mainly produced by nuclear plants, greenhouse gas emissions during use are lower than in other countries, but the amount of radioactive waste and the amount of fresh water required to cool the plants by evaporation are proportionally much higher. Every third party (Internet users, networks, data

---

26 Note that all the figures that follow come from this publication.

centers) consumes one-third of the energy during the phase of use of the Internet.

Should the quality (design, interface and use) of a site be forsaken? No, because it is absolutely possible to "boost" a site while reducing its carbon footprint. For this reason, Bordage proposed to include Web development and online services in an eco-design approach to reduce the environmental and economic impacts of software while improving their design and production. A total of 115 good practices are formulated and are divided between design (functional, graphic and technical aspects), templating (HTML, fonts, images, CSS), client code (JavaScript, DOM, animations, data exchange), server code (design, CMS, application server, database) and hosting (resources and content, physical and software infrastructure, cache), not to mention content (documents, emails, sounds, texts, videos).

This specialist is also very critical toward software publishers. Writing the same sentence consumes 128 times more memory with Office 2013 than with Office 2000, he warns. Another example is the end of maintenance for the Windows XP operating system announced in 2014 by Microsoft, which has prematurely discarded millions of computers. We might think that the situation differs for free software, but here too, the older and simpler versions are hardly kept longer. The following is the question some people rightly ask: would there be an agreement between computer manufacturers and software companies to favor an accelerated replacement of the equipment? As indicated by the WWF guide (2011, p. 8), "unlike an object, software does not wear out with time" and could be maintained over a longer time frame. And yet every new version of MS Office requires twice as many resources as the previous one. Thus, the power needed to write a text doubles every other year. Therefore, it takes 70 times more RAM with Windows 7 – Microsoft Office 2010 to write the same text than with

Windows 98 – Microsoft Office 97. This observation is not specific to Microsoft software; it is true for most publishers.

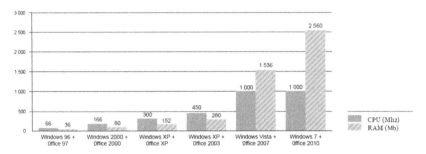

Figure 5.3. *Windows + Office: the minimum required configuration doubles every 2 years (source: 2010 GreenIT, Frédéric Bordage and Frédéric Lohier from Microsoft data)*

Having noted the absence of the environmental dimension and then proposed the need to consider the materiality of the immaterial to apprehend the energy consumption and the greenhouse gas production source of global warming, the impact of software and website design on their use has been examined. Finally, this work shall focus, between production and use, on obsolescence.

5.5. Injunctive, ecological and programmed obsolescence

Digital innovation fuels, as seen in Chapter 2, a product–service coupling that generates acute competition and unbridled productivism to renew hardware and application markets as quickly as possible. This process promotes the implementation of planned obsolescence, not only technical, but also injunctive. These practices involve technically shortening the life span of a product to force it to be renewed faster or more often than expected as well as a process that increases the production of electronic waste (also called e-waste). Marine Fabre and Wiebke Winkler (2010) perceived in planned obsolescence the symbol of a waste society. In France, since the adoption of the law on energy transition in July 2015, waste has become a crime, although it might not be easy to prove.

5.5.1. *Planned obsolescence*

It is important to remember that planned obsolescence is the process by which a product manufacturer will voluntarily shorten the life span of the product so as to favor its renewal. This obsolescence can be implemented in different ways: by voluntarily shortening the life span of a product or of its parts; making it impossible or too expensive to repair, for instance. It seems to have originated in the United States in the early 1920s with its goal being to shorten a product's life span. The first known case occurred in 1924 when the manufacturers of electric light bulbs created a secret association, a sort of cartel, known as Phoebus, also called the 1,000 hours Committee, in reference to the life span of the bulbs that they imposed. Thus, leaders and competitors agreed to voluntarily shorten the life span of incandescent light bulbs[27] without the knowledge of consumers and public authorities. This condemned the captive consumer to live subject to closer purchases, which shows that this approach does not aim for the sobriety or the longevity of the product.

This obsolescence can take various forms, as it will be shown, at the hardware or software level. Some printers, for example, contain chips programmed to block the printing mechanism once the number of predefined number of printed pages has been reached. Very recently in France, in September 2017, the association HOP (*Halte à l'obsolescence programée*, meaning "stop programmed obsolescence") relying on the consumer code that sanctions this type of

---

27 The second most famous case is nylon stockings.

practice has filed a complaint against manufacturers HP, Canon, Brother and Epson. One of the most resounding cases in the last few years is the inability to replace the used battery on the iPod. The end of life of the battery caused the end of life of the product. The only possible solution was to buy a new iPod. It can also result from a desired evolution of the connectors. Once again, Apple has distinguished itself by changing the iPhone 5 charger connector, making this model incompatible with other iPhones, as well as with iPads, iPods and docking stations. By proposing a state-of-the-art smartphone, this industrialist has forced customers, partners and accessory producers, as revealed by The Friends of the Earth (2012), to renew accessories, since none were compatible with the latest model. The same approach can be observed with phone or laptop chargers. Greenpeace conducted a study on mobile devices (smartphones, tablets, micro-laptops) to assess their compliance with a sustainable development model. Four criteria have been selected: the possibility to replace the battery, replacing the screen, access to specific tools and availability of spare parts. The study showed that, of the 44 best-selling models in recent years, only the Fairphone respects these criteria.

Another example known to every computer user: the installation and update of applications becomes impossible on equipment that is a little dated (only a few years old!). The computer owner is then forced to acquire a newer model if he/she wants to install new software versions. It is the same for downloading or accessing applications for smartphones. As these applications require increasing amounts of RAM to run, they require the possession of newer equipment, which feeds the renewal chain. It is important to note that regular updating of software is one of the main causes of equipment obsolescence, since any new version, any update, requires using more material resources in the hard disk, RAM or processor power.

5.5.2. *Injunctive obsolescence*

The vocation of injuctive obsolescence is, via advertising, marketing and communication strategies, to discredit an old product to favor the acquisition of a new one. The objective is to make the consumer believe that the product is obsolete, technically outdated and less fashionable in order to encourage consumers to buy a more "modern" product. This obsolescence contributes to the regular renewal of product ranges. Gunther Anders (2001) said, as early as 1956, that the mortality of products is necessary for the survival of production. Thus, disuse is programmed and planned. Apple has understood this well, which is clear from the range of iPhones between 2007 and 2013, that is, in just 5 years, eight iPhones have been marketed[28].

For considerations relating to purchasing power, ecological behavior or cultural or even ideological reasons, smartphone consumers have been moving for some time toward a still emerging market: re-employment, also known as "recommerce" or "reverse commerce", which refers to the recovery of used goods (free or paid), repackaging of the device and its remarketing. In other words, it is a second-hand market that differs from a classic second-hand market, since the equipment has been repackaged, and often guaranteed, before being resold. It has the advantage of increasing the duration of use of a product. This practice, still in its infancy, provides a service while reducing the production of goods and therefore the resources harvested and the waste associated. In France, experts agree that this concerns about 10% of the population who own a smartphone. Most often, this practice is developed via linking platforms and is part of the movement of the circular economy or the economy of functionality to replace the more

---

28 iPhone 2G (2007), iPhone 3G (2008), iPhone 3GS (2009), iPhone 4 (2010), iPhone 4S (2011), iPhone 5 (2012), iPhone 5C and 5S (2013).

traditional linear economy. This new orientation favors, among other factors, reuse (reusing an object that is in good condition for a purpose different from the intended use), repair (restoring damaged goods) or re-employment (giving a second life to objects that are still in good condition, but are no longer useful to their owner, through donation or resale). This results in longer durations of use. At present, re-employment is a new sector that is more environmentally friendly and emits lower levels of greenhouse gases.

5.5.3. *Ecological obsolescence*

Ecological obsolescence is also injunctive, but it seemed necessary to dissociate it from other forms, because it depends on environmental injunctions and recommendations. It has been increasingly asserting itself recently. The goal of industrialists, of the government, as well as of consumer associations, ecological collectives and some NGOs is to take advantage or promote awareness of the environmental facts to encourage consumers in the name of ecology to renew their equipment, so that they acquire less energy-intensive products that are more environmentally friendly. These actors are described by Howard S. Becker (1985) as "moral entrepreneurs", since the role of these organized groups is to promote norms and behaviors. They are, in a way, either creators of standards or defenders of established standards. Thus, most often, in a soft and benevolent way, these groups encourage the consumers to not wait for the end of life of their equipment to replace them with new ones.

This injunctive obsolescence may be a victim of the "rebound effect", which means, as seen previously, that the more the technological improvements increase the efficiency of using a resource, the more the total consumption of this resource will tend to increase, instead of decreasing. In other words, the progress made by technology is often annihilated by the change of behavior that it induces in the act of purchase and in the forms of use. To illustrate this, we take the most widely studied case. When renewing their television set, consumers were encouraged to buy a flat LED display instead of the good old CRT. The argument was that it was good for the planet as well as the buyers because these screens consume two to three times less energy. As prices have been steadily dropping, consumers have massively purchased larger flat screens and used them more than before, as they offer recognized, unprecedented contrasts, brightness and image quality, and in many cases, they are supplemented with additional equipment, such as home theaters. As a result, the new television sets consume more energy than the old ones. Consumer behavior and more intensive uses have eliminated the expected energy gain because there was not a simple substitution. The attractiveness of image quality encourages the viewer to use it more. In general, it is important to remember, as stated by Flipo and Gossart (2009), that when the energy intensity of an energy service is reduced, its price tends to decrease and its cost for the final consumer decreases. As a result, the consumer can either use the savings made to consume the service concerned with greater intensity or use it for other purposes[29]. This can be found, of course, at the DICT level. The decreasing cost of the equipment and the access to free services (informational, communicational and relational) and online software resources allow Internet users to save money in order to consume more intensively the services offered. Since these services are mostly free, it increases the intensity of use and generates more CO_2 and GHG, sources of global warming.

---

29 For further developments, see Flipo and Gossart (2009, pp. 163–178).

Conclusion

To conclude this third volume of the series "Computing and Connected Society", some perspectives on the hyperconnectivity situation will be presented. It seems useful, before addressing them, to return very briefly to the context and the main results of the analysis carried out so far.

After telematics (1970–1980) and the information superhighway (1990–2000), society as a whole is confronted with a third wave of social computerization, the digitization of society, which this time is massive and based on a communication system with platforms and social networks acting as pivots. The digitization of society refers to a global and transversal process, affecting all areas, sectors, socio-professional categories, work and home and each individual and at the heart of the most private and intimate relationships.

The creation of an offer accompanied by diversified services has contributed to a globalization of connection, to the diffusion of content by communication companies who hold a quasi-monopoly today and have enabled the United States of America to establish their hegemony. The importance of users, hundreds of millions of people, sometimes billions, depending on the applications, is at the heart of the strategies at work. The diffusion of uses on a planetary scale and their abundance cannot be understood without taking into account three main and unavoidable characteristics which mix business model and uses, thus forging an economy of hyperconnectivity, namely:

– a free mode of access and the use of socio-technological devices;

– an indirect mode of financing with two specificities, the sale of advertising space to advertisers and the promotion and marketing of personal data collected on the Web;

– a mode of activation, the unbridled solicitation, productivist for all, industrial, collective and individual users.

This socioeconomic model of "hyperconnectivity" generates a production, a display of the self, a visibility of singularities and an unsuspected circulation of data, while promoting unparalleled monitoring and diffuse social control. In the configuration studied, the government, being itself engaged, accompanies the digital economy which imposes the conditions of hyperconnectivity injunction, allowing the longevity of this socioeconomic model. Without this frantic global hyperconnectivity, the system could not optimally function or expand. Thus, free access for the user, its counterpart, advertising and sale of data, and the mode of activation by intense solicitations favor this connection, which in return leaves more traces and personal behavioral data. As freedom of expression, action, publication and exchange extends, social control extends with it by feeding on traces, often unbeknownst to users, of the content they left through Internet connection, through navigation and the willingness to voluntarily expose themselves. Given the importance acquired by these devices in relational, communicational or social practices, the concept of negotiated renunciation is a contribution to analyze the issues of hyperconnectivity. It makes it possible to understand that at every moment, the user must make choices between acceptance and subordination to obtain access to free services in return for having their data traced in order to feed the value chain relating to relational practices which are monitored, calculated and exploited by communication companies. For them, algorithmic innovations are a solution to identify and prescribe the uses, allowing the reinstation of a media diffusion, in contradiction with the first conception of decentralized networks based on the double TCP-IP protocol and the values of sharing and exchange. Let us not forget the neo-liberal inscription of this societal orientation, favoring empowerment, personalized staging and importing the entrepreneurial model in every activity, forcing people to stand out, to distinguish themselves and to compare themselves. This non-stop hyperconnectivity has a direct consequence which is too often and perhaps deliberately discarded or ignored in the name of a growing dematerialization of exchanges[1]. It impacts energy consumption more and more, which generates the production of carbon dioxide (CO_2) and greenhouse gases (GHGs), sources of global warming and climate change.

---

1 As announced with the arrival of computers with no "computer" allowing a connection from any medium, the processing unit being in the data centers. As proposed in late 2017 by the start-up, Blade, for the purchase of a modem and a monthly subscription. See AFP, "Blade the start-up hurried to put the computer in the cloud", *Le Point*, 22 November 2017, available at: http://www.lepoint.fr/economie/blade-la-start-up-pressee-qui-veut-mettre-l-ordinateur-dans-le-nuage-22-11-2017-2174362_28.php.

A question arises: what could happen to this model of hyperconnectivity that seems too unsustainable, although it continues to expand and enlist more users? To try to answer this question, we propose some reflections around three dialectical perspectives: emancipation – technological, social and economic subordination; exhaustion of the free model – reconfiguration; and energy bomb – climatic impasse.

Emancipation – technical, social and economic subordination

As seen previously, users have to deal with massive data flows as part of the process of contemporary digital appropriation, leading to the need to benefit from prescriptions and recommendations in order to identify themselves and continue their network activities. Thus, they are ready to accept algorithms that trace their uses, in a negotiated renunciation. Let us now attend to a new form of dissemination, one that is less new, that would hide its marks to maintain the user experience and generate social innovations to exploit. We would be faced with a form of limited subordination by voluntary renunciation. The lure is at its peak when users and distributors come together to produce services and goods, making up the business model, allowing the very existence of "pure player" companies or giants of the communication industry. Users would be both hostages and protagonists of developments in the economic value of social activities. The citizen-consumer user, who is valued in these network and media environments, can then abandon the debate around these by seizing them, in favor of bringing economic, cultural globalization up to standard, even instrumentalizing social activities for commercial purposes. As a result, users of digital networks would not emancipate themselves, while domination would persist. While reproducing the context in which uses evolve, they would be part of an ecosystem of domination in which power and influence would prevail, losing the opportunity to deploy digital technologies with emancipation as a goal. However, freedom of action persists, since renunciation is not alienation, and the situation tends to open to a contemporary subordination to hyperconnectivity's injunctions of domination.

Free model exhaustion – reconfiguration

Another perspective that can be evoked is that without waiting for the intervention of regulatory bodies emanating from public authorities or professional regulatory authorities, forms of resistance are organized. Exasperated by the practices developed by communication industrialists, some users want to protect themselves (like in a consistent way in Germany and Scandinavia) against untimely investigations in their privacy by configuring their browser as much as possible to no longer be "tracked" or by installing ad blockers, software meant to prevent the display of invasive advertising (bear in mind that in order to increase their revenues, more and more websites tend to give priority to displaying advertisements on the content itself), disrupting the economy of advertising space sales, but also the value creation and marketing of personal data recovered and then sold. Others limit[2] cookies as much as possible, moving to anonymous networks like Tor, or using alternative hosts, social networks and search engines, whose business model is based on revenues expected from sponsored links, but these are not displayed, according to them, by associating query and user profile. The tendency of this practice to expand and strengthen itself could disrupt

---

2 See the CECIL association's practical fact sheets, Centre d'études sur la citoyenneté, l'informatisation et les libertés, available at: https://www. lececil.org/node/7687.

the current socioeconomic model, unless industrialists and advertisers find solutions as the following examples seem to indicate. Indeed, faced with the decline in advertising revenue generated by these practices, communication industrialists retaliate by offering ad blocking software, but these are affiliated with advertising groups, allowing only the display of their own advertisements, and other publishers of ad blocking software accept, for a fee, to let "acceptable" ads (on a white list) through. Some sites force the user to disable their ad blocker software if they want to view their webpage content. This is unless the offered strategy is based on a differentiated offer combining a freemium offer, with free access, but with various restrictions (of features, access, etc.) or if they encourage users to purchase a paid version, a premium offer with a higher added value through paid access.

Energy bomb – climate impasse

Despite the search for better equipment efficiency and energy control policies, the extent and intensity of this hyperconnectivity, in full growth, largely annihilates the expected energy gains. As for the rebound effect, it participates more and more, contrary to what was hoped, to the increase in energy consumption. Let us not forget the importance taken by 4G and soon 5G in the field of telephony and mobile Internet, and the use of video by advertisers which is very energy-intensive in terms of bandwidth, all of which increase the digital weight of exchanges, requiring significant electrical energy, and an increase in consumption. What seems most important to remember is the massive development of Internet access and therefore the increasing share of users in areas that are still little or not concerned today. The demographic shock associated with the multiplication and the intensity of uses would favor tomorrow's energy bomb which would have three consequences: the multiplication of electrical production sites, the inequitable distribution of capacity and electric power and the use of fossil fuels generating CO_2 and greenhouse gases, sources of global warming. We are in this area at best before a climatic impasse, at worst before even stronger harm is done to the climate. For some people, nuclear energy seems to be an essential element in the fight against global warming, since this energy source can lower the level of fossil fuels. However, because of the inherent risks of this means of electricity production, the extreme difficulty in storing radioactive waste for hundreds or even thousands of years, the vast majority of countries gave up this energy, also due to the colossal costs for constructing and dismantling nuclear plants. This element is to be linked to the continuous price drop of renewable energies (photovoltaic and wind). For example, in India, where the use of DICT is increasingly important, solar power production (photovoltaic panels) is more competitive than producing electricity with coal. Unfortunately, the deployment of renewable energy is much too slow. As a result, the increase in electricity capacity for the use of DICT greatly depends on fossil carbon energy, coal and, to a lesser extent, other energy sources, such as oil and gas. Also, 77% of electricity in this country comes from coal. Keep in mind that because of significant losses between primary energy (before the transformation of raw materials into energy), its transportation and the consumption of final energy, only a quarter of the electric energy produced can be truly consumed. It is therefore necessary to produce a lot and to pollute in order to consume this energy. As for some countries, turning to gas for electricity production is not much better since its contribution to global warming would be much higher than the IPCC estimated[3]. Thus, efforts to

3 Intergovernmental Panel on Climate Change, 5th Report, Geneva, 2014.

reduce CO_2 emissions could be canceled in the absence of methane (CH4) reduction[4].

We have just proposed an analysis of the economic, social and environmental issues of hyperconnectivity. After a socio-historic approach developed in volume 1 by André Vitalis to address the computerization of society, the second volume allowed Laurent Gayard to address the darknet in a geopolitical dimension. This third volume discussed the consequences of hyperconnectivity, industrialization and the commodification of social interactions. We hope to continue the work in the "Computers and Connected Society" series with the subject of legal issues.

---

4 CO_2 is not the only greenhouse gas. If it represents more than half of the gases contributing to global warming, a third is attributable to methane (40% of agriculture and 60% of the energy system). The characteristic of methane is that it degrades after a dozen years into other greenhouse gases.

References

ADEME, Analyse comparée des impacts environnementaux de la communication par voie électronique, study led by Bio Intelligence Service, July 2011.

ADEME, Les TIC quels impacts?, Guide, 2011.

ADEME, Face cachée du numérique (La). Réduire les impacts du numérique sur l'environnement, Pratical guide, June 2017.

ADEME, ADN OUEST, KALITERRE, EASYVIRT, A2JV, Consommation énergétique des équipements informatiques en milieu professionnel, White paper, Summary of "Conso IT" study, p. 58, November 2015.

AGAMBEN G., *Qu'est-ce qu'un dispositif?*, Payot & Rivages, Paris, 2007.

AKRICH M., "Les objets techniques et leurs utilisateurs. De la conception à l'action", *Raisons Pratiques*, no. 4, pp. 35–57, available at: http://hal.archives-ouvertes.fr/docs/00/08/17/31/PDF/93raison_pratique.pdf, 1993.

AKRICH M., CALLON M., LATOUR B., *Sociologie de la traduction. Textes fondateurs*, Presses des Mines de Paris, Paris, 2006.

ANDERS G., *L'obsolescence de l'homme*, vol. 1, Éditions de l'Encyclopédie des Nuisances, Paris, 2002.

ANDERSON C., *Makers: la nouvelle révolution industrielle*, Pearson, London, 2012.

BARATS C. (ed.), *Manuel d'analyse du Web*, Armand Colin, Paris, 2013.

BARBROOK R., "La liberté de l'hypermédia. Une réponse à John Perry Barlow", in BLONDEAU O. (ed.), *Libres enfants du savoir numérique*, pp. 55–76, Éditions de l'éclat, Paris, 2000.

BECKER H.S., *Outsiders*, Éditions Métailié, Paris, 1985.

BENGHOZI P.J., PARIS T., "De l'intermédiation à la prescription: le cas de l'audiovisuel", *Revue Française de Gestion*, available at: https://halshs.archives-ouvertes.fr/hal-00262496/document, vol. 29, no. 402, pp. 205–227, January/February 2003.

BENGHOZI P.J., PARIS T., "The economics and business models of prescription in the Internet", in BROUSSEAU E., CURIEN N. (eds), *Internet and Digital Economics: Principles, Methods and Applications*, pp. 291–310, Cambridge University Press, Cambridge, available at: https://hal.archives-ouvertes.fr/hal-00263198, 2007.

BENJAMIN W., *L'œuvre d'art à l'époque de sa reproductibilité technique*, Éditions Allia, Paris, 2003.

BERRY G., *Pourquoi et comment le monde devient numérique: leçons inaugurales au Collège de France*, Collège de France/Fayard, Paris, 2008.

BERTHOUD F., *Écoconception Web: les 115 bonnes pratiques*, Eyrolles, Paris, 2015.

BOLTANSKI L., CHIAPELLO E., *Le nouvel esprit du capitalisme*, Gallimard, Paris, 1999.

BORDAGE F., *Écoconception Web: les 115 bonnes pratiques*, Eyrolles, Paris, 2015.

BOULLIER D., "Du bon usage d'une critique du modèle diffusionniste: discussion-prétexte des concepts d'Everett Rogers", *Réseaux*, vol. 7, no. 36, pp. 31–51, available at: http://www.persee.fr/web/revues/home/prescript/article/reso_0751-7971_1989_num_7_36_1351?_Prescripts_Search_isPortlet Ouvrage=false, 1989.

BOURDIEU P., *La distinction. Critique sociale du jugement*, Éditions de Minuit, Paris, 1979.

BOURDIEU P., *Le Sens pratique*, Éditions de Minuit, Paris, 1980a.

BOURDIEU P., *Questions de sociologie*, Éditions de Minuit, Paris, 1980b.

BOURDIEU P., *Raisons pratiques sur la théorie de l'action*, Le Seuil, Paris, 1994.

BOURDIEU P., *Science de la science et réflexivité*, Raisons d'agir, Paris, 2001.

BRAUDEL F., *Civilisation matérielle, Économie et Capitalisme. XVe-XVIIIe siècle*, 3 volumes, LGF/Livre de poche, Paris, 2000.

BREUIL H., BURETTE D., CUEUGNIET J. *et al*.,Tic et Développement durable, Report, Ministry of Ecology, Energy, Sustainable Development and Spatial Planning, December 2008.

CARDON D., "Le design de la visibilité. Un essai de cartographie du Web 2.0", *Réseaux*, vol. 6, no. 152, pp. 93–137, 2008.

CARDON D., *À quoi rêvent les algorithmes. Nos vies à l'heure du big data*, La République des idées/Le Seuil, Paris, 2015.

CARRÉ D., "Antiope une fausse bonne idée", in LACROIX J.-G., TREMBLAY G., MIÈGE B. (eds), *De la télématique aux autoroutes électroniques. Le grand projet reconduit*, PUQ-PUG, Montreal, 1994.

CARRÉ D., "Des dégâts du progrès… au marketing de l'usage. Revirement de perspective en matière de critique sociale dans le champ informatique et société", *Terminal – Technologie de l'information, culture & société*, pp. 91–100, December 2005.

CARRÉ D., "Trois postures communicationnelles en santé: désingularisation, culpabilisation et imposition", in ROUTIER C., d'ARRIPE A. (eds), *Communication & santé. Enjeux contemporains*, pp. 173–182, Presses universitaires du Septentrion, Villeneuve d'Ascq, 2010.

CARRÉ D., "Étudier les usages. Est-ce encore nécessaire ?", in VIDAL G. (ed.), *La sociologie des usages continuités et transformations*, pp. 63–85, Hermès Science-Lavoisier, Paris, 2012.

CARRÉ D., "Approche critique et techniques numériques d'infocommunication: Vers la prise en compte d'une nouvelle dimension?", *80ᵉ Congrès de l'ACFAS*, Montreal, Canada, available at: http://www.cricis.uqam.ca/IMG/pdf/ActesColloque Ou-_en_-est-la-critique-en-communication_Gricis2012_Reduit.pdf, 1–11 May 2012.

CARRÉ D., LACROIX J.G. (eds), *La santé et les autoroutes de l'information: la greffe informatique*, L'Harmattan, Paris, 2001.

CARRÉ D., PANICO R., "De l'usage du marketing au marketing de l'usage: la finalité de la notion d'usages revisitée", *Penser les usages*, Arcachon, France, 27–29 May 1997.

CARRÉ D., PANICO R., "Le contrôle social à l'heure des technologies de mobilité et de connectivité. Du fichage ciblé des individus au traçage continu des agissements", *Terminal – Technologie de l'information, culture & société*, no. 108, pp. 17–31, 2011.

CARRÉ D., PANICO R., "Du fichage subi à l'affichage de soi. Eléments pour une approche communicationnelle du contrôle social", in PROULX S., KLEIN A. (eds), *Connexions. Communication numérique et lien social*, pp. 269–283, Presses universitaires de Namur, Namur, 2012a.

CARRÉ D., PANICO R., "L'"affichage de soi" comme puissance d'agir: contrôle social et enjeux éthiques à l'heure de l'hyperconnectivité", in PROULX S., MILLETTE M., HEATON L. (eds), *Médias sociaux. Enjeux pour la communication*, pp. 61–79, Presses de l'Université du Québec, Québec, 2012b.

CARRÉ D., PANICO R., "Puissance d'agir à l'ère du Web social", in ROJAS E. (ed.), *Réseaux socionumériques et médiations humaines. Le social est-il soluble dans le Web?*, pp. 177–197, Hermès Science-Lavoisier, Paris, 2013.

CARRÉ D., VÉTOIS J., "Contrôle social et techniques numériques", *tic&société*, vol. 10, no. 1, available at: http://ticetsociete. revues.org/1973, 2016.

CASILLI A., *Les liaisons numériques*, Le Seuil, Paris, 2010.

CASTORIADIS C., *L'institution imaginaire de la société*, Le Seuil, Paris, 1975.

CERTEAU M. (DE), *L'invention du quotidien, I: Arts de faire*, Gallimard, Paris, 1990.

CHAMBAT P., "Usages des technologies de l'information et de la communication (TIC): évolution des problématiques", *Technologies de l'Information et Société*, vol. 6, no. 3, pp. 249–270, 1994.

CHARBONNEAU B., *Dimanche et lundi*, Denoël, Paris, 1966.

CHOMSKY N., "Les exploits de la propagande", in CHOMSKY N., MCCHESNEY R.W. (eds), *Propagande, médias et démocratie*, pp. 13–67, Écosociété, Montreal, 2004.

CITTON Y. (ed.), *L'économie de l'attention. Nouvel horizon du capitalisme?*, La Découverte, Paris, 2014.

COADY D., PERRY I., SEARS L. *et al.*, How large are global energy subsidies?, Report, FMI, May 2015.

DEBORD G., *La société du spectacle*, Gallimard, Paris, 1992.

DELMAS-MARTY M., MASSIT-FOLLÉA F., "La démocratisation des savoirs", *Rue Descartes*, no. 55, pp. 59–69, 2007/1.

DUDEN B., "Illich, seconde période", *Esprit*, August–September 2010.

DURKHEIM É., *Éléments d'une théorie sociale*, vol. 1, Éditions de Minuit, Paris, 1975.

EIGLIER P., LANGEARD E., *Servuction: le marketing des services*, Édiscience, Paris, 1987.

ELIAS N., *Qu'est-ce que la sociologie?*, Éditions de l'Aube, La Tour d'Aigues, 1991.

ELLUL J., *La technique ou l'enjeu du siècle*, Economica, Paris, 1990.

ELLUL J., *Le système technicien*, Calmann-Lévy, Paris, 2004.

ENGUEHARD C., PANICO R., "Technologies et usages de l'anonymat sur Internet", *Terminal*, no. 105, 2010.

FABRE M., WIEBKE W., L'obsolescence programmée, symbole de la société de gaspillage. Le cas des produits électriques et électroniques, Report, CNID, 2010.

FAUCHEUX S., HUE C., NICOALAÏ S., *Tic et développement durable. Les conditions du succès*, De Boeck, Brussels, 2010.

FAYON D., *Made in $ilicon Valley. Du numérique en Amérique*, Pearson, London, 2017.

FLICHY P., *Les industries de l'imaginaire. Pour une analyse économique des médias*, PUG, Grenoble, 1991.

FLICHY P., *L'imaginaire d'Internet*, La Découverte, Paris, 2001.

FLIPO F., DOBRÉ M., MICHOT M., *La face cachée du numérique. L'impact environnemental des nouvelles technologies*, L'échappée, Montreuil, 2013.

FLIPO F., GOSSART C., "Infrastructure numérique et environnement. L'impossible domestication de l'effet rebond", *Terminal*, nos 103–104, pp. 163–177, 2009.

FOEGLE J.-P., "L'État de la surveillance au régime sec: la CJUE renforce la prohibition de la surveillance "de masse"", *La Revue des droits de l'homme*, available at: http.//revdh.revues.org/2966, 2017.

FOREST D., *Abécédaire de la société de surveillance*, Éditions Syllepse, Paris, 2009.

FOUCAULT M., *Surveiller et punir*, Gallimard, Paris, 1975.

FOUCAULT M., *Dits et écrits*, vol. 2, Gallimard, Paris, 1982.

FOUCAULT M., *Le souci de soi*, Gallimard, Paris, 1984.

FOUCAULT M., *Dits et écrits*, vol. 3, Gallimard, Paris, 1994.

FOUCAULT M., *Naissance de la biopolitique*, Le Seuil, Paris, 2004.

GARNHAM N., "Contribution to a Political Economy of Mass-Communication", in DURHAM M.G., KELLNER D.M. (eds), *Media and Cultural studies: Keyworks*, Blackwell Publishing Ltd, Oxford, available at: https://we.riseup.net/assets/102142/appadurai.pdf, 2006.

GAYARD L., *Darknet: Geopolitics and Uses*, ISTE Ltd, London and John Wiley & Sons, New York, 2018.

GENSOLLEN M., "La création de valeur sur Internet", *Réseaux*, no. 97, pp. 15–76, 1999.

GIEC (GROUPE INTERGOUVERNEMENTAL SUR L'ÉVOLUTION DU CLIMAT), 5ᵉ rapport, 2014.

GLANZ J., "The cloud factories: power, pollution and the Internet", *New York Times*, 22 September 2012.

GODARD O., "Le climato-scepticisme médiatique en France: un sophisme moderne", *Écologie & Politique*, no. 45, pp. 46–69, 2012.

GOFFMAN E., *Les cadres de l'expérience*, Éditions de Minuit, Paris, 1991.

GOLDHABER M.H, "The attention economy and the net", *First Monday*, vol. 2, nos 4–7, available at: httpp://firstmonday.org/, April 1997.

GORNAL W., STREBULAEV I.A., Squaring venture capital valuations with reality, document de recherche nos 17–29, available at: https://ssrn.com/abstract=2955455, 12 July 2017.

GREENPEACE, Votre Cloud est-il Net ?, Brochure, April 2012.

HABERMAS J., *La technique et la science comme "idéologie"*, Gallimard, Paris, 1990.

HALL S., "Codage-Décodage", *Réseaux*, vol. 1, no. 1, pp. 27–39, 1997.

HORKHEIMER M., ADORNO T.W., *La dialectique de la raison*, pp. 129–176, Gallimard, Paris, 1974.

HUITEMA C., "Quel avenir pour l'Internet", in ARCHIMBAUD J.L. (ed.), *L'Internet professionnel*, pp. 8–11, CNRS Éditions, Paris, 1995.

HUTCHINS E., "Comment le "cockpit" se souvient de ses vitesses", *Sociologie du travail*, no. 4, pp. 451–473, 1994.

ILLICH Y., *Énergie et équité,* Le Seuil, Paris, 1975.

ILLICH Y., *Le travail fantôme*, Le Seuil, Paris, 1981.

ILLICH Y., *Œuvres complètes*, vol. 1, Fayard, Paris, 2003.

ILLICH Y., *La perte des sens*, Fayard, Paris, 2004.

ILLICH Y., *Œuvres complètes*, vol. 2, Fayard, Paris, 2005.

INNIS H.A., *The bias of communication*, University of Toronto Press, Toronto, 1971.

JACQUINOT-DELAUNAY G., MONNOYER L. (eds), "Le dispositif. Entre usage et concept", *Hermès, La Revue*, no. 25, 1999.

JAURÉGUIBERRY F., PROULX S., *Usages et technologies de communication*, Éditions Érès, Toulouse, 2011.

JAUSS H.R., *Pour une esthétique de la réception*, Gallimard, Paris, 1978.

JOUËT J., "Pratiques de communication et figure de la médiation", *Réseaux*, vol. 11, no. 60, pp. 99–120, 1993.

JOUËT J., "Retour critique sur la sociologie des usages", *Réseaux*, vol. 18, no. 100, pp. 487–521, 2000.

JOUËT J., "Des usages de la télématique aux Internet Studies", in DENOUËL J., GRANJON F. (eds), *Communiquer à l'ère numérique. Regards croisés sur la sociologie des usages*, pp. 45–90, Presses des Mines, Paris, 2011.

JOUVENEL B. (DE), *Arcadie. Essais sur le mieux vivre*, Gallimard, Paris, 2002.

KATZ E., "Lire la réception à travers le modèle des effets limités. Actualité de Lazarsfeld", in MÉADEL C. (ed.), *La réception*, CNRS Éditions, Paris, 2009.

KELLNER D., "Overcoming the divide: Cultural Studies and Political Economy", in FERGUSON M., GOLDING P. (eds), *Cultural Studies in Question*, pp. 102–120, Sage, London, 1997.

KESSOUS E., *L'attention au monde. Sociologie des données personnelles à l'ère numérique*, Armand Colin, Paris, 2012.

LA BOÉTIE E. (DE), *Discours de la servitude volontaire*, Éditions Mille et une nuits, Paris, 1995.

LAMY A., CARRÉ D. (eds), *Temps, temporalité(s) et dispositifs de médiation*, L'Harmattan, Paris, 2017.

LAPEYRONNIE D., "Le pouvoir de l'expérience", in OULC'HEN H. (ed.), *Usages de Foucault*, pp. 207–229, PUF, Paris, 2013.

LA REVUE DURABLE, "Les Technologies de l'information et de la communication et l'impératif de sobriété", no. 49, June–July–August, 2013.

LA REVUE DURABLE, "Libérons-nous des énergies fossiles !", no. 55, August–September–October, 2015.

LATOUR B., WOOLGAR S., *La Vie de laboratoire: la Production des faits scientifiques,* La Découverte, Paris, 1988.

LAVAL C., "L'entreprise, comme nouvelle forme de gouvernement. Usages et mésusages de Michel Foucault", in OULC'HEN H. (ed.), *Usages de Foucault*, pp. 143–158, PUF, Paris, 2013.

LE CROSNIER H., "De l'immatériel énergivore à l'énergie sociale des réseaux de communications", *EcoRev*, no. 37, pp. 72–77, 2011.

LE CROSNIER H., *En-communs: une introduction aux communs de la connaissance*, C&F Éditions, Caen, 2015.

LEFEBVRE H., *Méthodologie des sciences*, Anthropos, Paris, 2002.

LEFEBVRE H., *Critique de la vie quotidienne. Introduction*, vol. 1, L'Arche, Paris, 1958.

LEFEBVRE H., *Critique de la vie quotidienne. Fondements d'une sociologie de la quotidienneté*, vol. 2, L'Arche, Paris, 1961.

LEFEBVRE H., *Critique de la vie quotidienne. De la modernité au modernisme (Pour une métaphilosophie du quotidien)*, vol. 3, L'Arche, Paris, 1981.

LES AMIS DE LA TERRE, "La sortie du nouvel iPhone 5: l'obsolescence programmée en série", available at: http://amisdelaterre.org, 2012.

LES ASSOCIÉS D'EIM, *Les dirigeants face au changement*, Éditions du Huitième jour, Paris, 2004.

MANN S. *et al.*, "Sousveillance: inventing and using wearable computing devices for data collection in surveillance environnement", *Surveillance and Society*, vol. 1, no. 3, 2003.

MASSIT-FOLLÉA F., "Usages des Technologies de l'Information et de la Communication: acquis et perspectives de la recherche", *Le Français dans le Monde*, Special edition, available at: http://c2so.ens-lyon.fr/IMG/pdf/rechercheUsages_FMF_LFM.pdf, 2002.

MASSIT-FOLLÉA F., "Usages et Gouvernance de l'Internet: pour une convergence sociopolitique", in VIDAL G. (ed.), *La sociologie des usages: continuités et transformations*, pp. 153–178, Hermes Science-Lavoisier, Paris, 2012.

MASSIT-FOLLÉA F., DELMAS R., "La gouvernance d'Internet", *Les Cahiers du Numérique*, vol. 3, no. 2, 2002.

MATTELART A., NEVEU E., "Cultural studies' stories. La domestication d'une pensée sauvage?", *Réseaux*, vol. 14, no. 80, pp. 11–58, available at: http://www.persee.fr/web/revues/home/prescript/article/reso_0751-7971_1996_num_14_80_3799, 1996.

MATTELART A., NEVEU E., *Introduction aux cultural studies*, La Découverte, Paris, 2003.

MATTELART A., VITALIS A., *Le profilage des populations. Du livret ouvrier au cybercontrôle*, La Découverte, Paris, 2014.

MCCHESNEY R., "Internet et la révolution numérique", in CHOMSKY N., MCCHESNEY W.R (eds), *Propagande, médias et démocratie*, pp. 137–143, Écosociété, Montreal, 2004.

MIÈGE B., "L'économie politique de la communication", *Hermès, La Revue*, no. 38, pp. 46–54, available at: http://documents.irevues.inist.fr/bitstream/handle/2042/9423/HERMES_2004_38_46.pdf; jsessionid=5B8A0D8B46A3641AB6B716A159B21BA6?sequence =1, 2004.

MIÈGE B., *La société conquise par la communication: tome 3, les tic entre innovation technique et ancrage social*, PUG, Grenoble, 2017.

MIÈGE B., TREMBLAY G., "Pour une grille de lecture du développement des techniques de l'information et de la communication", *Sciences de la Société*, no. 47, p. 13, May 1999.

MILLS M.P., The cloud begings with coal. Big data, big Networks, Big infrastructure, and big power. An overview of the electricity used by the global digital ecosystem, Digital Power Group, August 2013.

OULC'HEN H. (ed.), *Usages de Foucault*, PUF, Paris, 2013.

PAOLETTI F., *L'homme et l'ordinateur. Les enjeux de l'informatisation de la société*, L'Harmattan, Paris, 2003.

PAPILLOUD C., *La société collaborative*, L'Harmattan, Paris, 2007.

PAQUOT T., *Introduction à Ivan Illich*, La Découverte, Paris, 2012.

PARIS T., "Des industries culturelles aux industries créatives: un changement de paradigme salutaire?", *Tic&Société*, vol. 4, no. 2, available at: https://ticetsociete.revues.org/871, 2010.

PERRIAULT J., *La logique de l'usage, Essai sur les machines à communiquer*, Flammarion, Paris, 1989.

PROULX S., "La construction sociale des objets informationnels: matériaux pour une ethnographie des usages", *Comprendre les usages d'Internet*, available at: http://barthes.ens.fr/atelier/articles/proulx2000.html, Paris, France, 3–4 December 1999.

PROULX S., "Usages des technologies de l'information et de la communication: reconsidérer le champ d'étude", *12ᵉ congrès de la Société française des sciences de l'information et de la communication (SFSIC)*, available at: http://www.er.uqam.ca/nobel/grmnob/drupal5.1/static/textes/proulx_SFSIC2001.pdf, Paris, France, 10–13 January 2001.

PROULX S., GOLDENBERG A., "Internet et la culture de la gratuité", *Revue du Mauss*, no. 35, pp. 273–287, 2009.

PROULX S., POISSANT L., SÉNÉCAL M. (eds), *Communautés virtuelles: penser et agir en réseau*, Presses de l'Université de Laval, Québec, 2006.

PROULX S., SÉNÉCAL M., "L'interactivité technique, simulacre d'interaction sociale et de démocratie?", *TIS*, vol. 7, no. 2, pp. 239–255, 1995.

RALLET A., "Une économie de la communication?", *Hermès, La Revue*, no. 44, pp. 169–177, available at: https://www.cairn.info/revue-hermes-la-revue-2006-1-page-169.htm, 2006.

RANCIÈRE J., *Le spectateur émancipé*, La fabrique éditions, Paris, 2008.

RICŒUR P., *Temps et récit*, Le Seuil, Paris, 1983.

RIFKIN J., *La nouvelle société au coût marginal zéro: l'internet des objets, l'émergence des communaux collaboratifs et l'éclipse du capitalisme*, Actes Sud, Arles, 2016.

ROBINSON M., "Concevoir pour des utilisations imprévues", *Réseaux*, no. 69, pp. 121–138, available at: http://www.enssib.fr/autres-sites/reseaux-cnet/69/05-robison.pdf, 1995.

ROSA H., *Accélération, une critique sociale du temps*, La Découverte, Paris, 2010.

SEARLS D., *The intention economy: When customers take change*, Business Review Press, Harvard, 2012.

SIMMEL G., *Sociologie et épistémologie*, PUF, Paris, 1991.

SIMON H.A., "Design organizations for an information-rich world", in GREENBERG M. (ed.), *Computers, communication and the public interest*, The John Hopkins Press, Baltimore, 1971.

SUPIOT A., *La Gouvernance par les nombres: cours au Collège de France (2012–2014)*, Fayard, Paris, 2015.

SMYTHE D., "Communications: blindpost of Western marxism", *Canadian Journal of political ans social theory*, vol. 1, no. 3, 1977.

SYNTEC, Datacenters et développement durable. État de l'art et perspectives, Green book, London, available at: https://syntec-numerique.fr/sites/default/files/Documents/livre_vert_vol.5_datacenters_etat_de_lart_et_perspectives.pdf, 2011.

TISSERON S., *L'intimité surexposée*, Ramsay, Paris, 2001.

VAIDHYANATHAN S., "Naked in the nonopticon: surveillance and marketing combined strip away our privacy", *The Chronicle of Higher Education*, vol. 54, no. 23, February 2008.

VALENDUC G., "L'évaluation sociétale des TIC: quelques réflexions sur 25 ans de technology assessment", *tic&société*, vol. 1, no. 1, available at: http://journals.openedition.org/ticetsociete/265, 2007.

VALENDUC G., VENDRAMIN P., *Le travail à distance dans la société de l'information*, Éditions EVO, Brussels, 1997.

VÉTOIS J., "Le développement durable à l'épreuve des TIC", *Terminal*, nos 106–107, 2011.

VIDAL G., "Mygale-bêta: crise et décision sur l'Internet", *Terminal*, no. 78, pp. 51–77, 1999.

VIDAL G., "Internautes citoyens et consommateurs", in LACROIX J.G., TREMBLAY G. (eds), *2001 Bogues, globalisme et pluralisme: usages des TIC*, pp. 325–339, Presses de l'Université de Laval, Québec, 2003.

VIDAL G., "Expérimenter l'interactivité", in VIEIRA L., PINÈDE-WOJCIECHOWSKI N. (eds), *Enjeux et usages des T.I.C.: aspects sociaux et culturels: actes du colloque du 22-24 septembre 2005 à l'Université Bordeaux Montaigne*, pp. 347–353, Presses universitaires de Bordeaux, Pessac, 2005.

VIDAL G., "Le renoncement négocié. Pour une analyse dialectique des usages des technologies interactive", HDR thesis, Bordeaux University 3, 2010.

VIDAL G. (ed.), *La sociologie des usages: continuités et transformations*, Hermes Science-Lavoisier, Paris, 2012.

VIDAL G., "Présentation. Instabilité et permanence des usages numériques", *Les Cahiers du Numérique*, vol. 9, no. 2, pp. 9–46, 2013.

VIDAL G., MABILLOT V., "Culture de la crise, adaptation et résistance des utilisateurs des réseaux peer-to-peer", *Terminal*, nos 97–98, pp. 85–94, 2006.

VITALIS A. (ed.), *Médias et nouvelles technologies de communication. Pour une sociopolitique des usages*, Apogée, Rennes, 1994.

VITALIS A., *The Uncertain Digital Revolution*, ISTE Ltd, London and John Wiley & Sons, New York, 2016.

VON HIPPEL E., "Horizontal Innovation Networks by and for Users", *Industrial and Corporate Change*, vol. 16, no. 2, pp. 293–315, 2007.

WEBER M., *Économie et Société. Les catégories de la sociologie*, Pocket, Paris, 1995.

WEBER M., *L'éthique protestante et l'esprit du capitalisme*, Gallimard, Paris, 2003.

WILSON K.G., *Technologies of Control. The New Interactive Media for the Home*, University of Wisconsin Press, Madison, 1988.

WORLD BANK, Rapport sur le développement dans le monde. Les dividendes du numérique, Report, available at: http://www.worldbank.org/wdr2016, 2016.

WRIGHT MILLS C., *L'imagination sociologique*, La Découverte, Paris, 2006.

WWF, Guide pour un système d'information éco-responsable, Guide, 2011.

Index

Other titles from

in

Information Systems, Web and Pervasive Computing

2018

ARDUIN Pierre-Emmanuel
Insider Threats
(Advances in Information Systems Set – Volume 10)

CHAMOUX Jean-Pierre
The Digital Era 1: Big Data Stakes

CARMÈS Maryse
Digital Organizations Manufacturing: Scripts, Performativity and
Semiopolitics
(Intellectual Technologies Set – Volume 5)

DOUAY Nicolas
Urban Planning in the Digital Age
(Intellectual Technologies Set – Volume 6)

FABRE Renaud, BENSOUSSAN Alain
The Digital Factory for Knowledge: Production and Validation of Scientific
Results

GAUDIN Thierry, LACROIX Dominique, MAUREL Marie-Christine, POMEROL
Jean-Charles
Life Sciences, Information Sciences

GAYARD Laurent
Darknet: Geopolitics and Uses
(Computing and Connected Society Set – Volume 2)

IAFRATE Fernando
Artificial Intelligence and Big Data: The Birth of a New Intelligence
(Advances in Information Systems Set – Volume 8)

LE DEUFF Olivier
Digital Humanities: History and Development
(Intellectual Technologies Set – Volume 4)

MANDRAN Nadine
Traceable Human Experiment Design Research: Theoretical Model and
Practical Guide
(Advances in Information Systems Set – Volume 9)

PIVERT Olivier
NoSQL Data Models: Trends and Challenges

ROCHET Claude
Smart Cities: Reality or Fiction

SEDKAOUI Soraya
Data Analytics and Big Data

SZONIECKY Samuel
Ecosystems Knowledge: Modeling and Analysis Method for Information and
Communication
(Digital Tools and Uses Set – Volume 6)

2017

BOUHAÏ Nasreddine, SALEH Imad
Internet of Things: Evolutions and Innovations
(Digital Tools and Uses Set – Volume 4)

DUONG Véronique
Baidu SEO: Challenges and Intricacies of Marketing in China

LESAS Anne-Marie, MIRANDA Serge
The Art and Science of NFC Programming
(Intellectual Technologies Set – Volume 3)

LIEM André
Prospective Ergonomics
(Human-Machine Interaction Set – Volume 4)

MARSAULT Xavier
Eco-generative Design for Early Stages of Architecture
(Architecture and Computer Science Set – Volume 1)

REYES-GARCIA Everardo
The Image-Interface: Graphical Supports for Visual Information
(Digital Tools and Uses Set – Volume 3)

REYES-GARCIA Everardo, BOUHAÏ Nasreddine
Designing Interactive Hypermedia Systems
(Digital Tools and Uses Set – Volume 2)

SAÏD Karim, BAHRI KORBI Fadia
Asymmetric Alliances and Information Systems:Issues and Prospects
(Advances in Information Systems Set – Volume 7)

SZONIECKY Samuel, BOUHAÏ Nasreddine
Collective Intelligence and Digital Archives: Towards Knowledge
Ecosystems
(Digital Tools and Uses Set – Volume 1)

2016

BEN CHOUIKHA Mona
Organizational Design for Knowledge Management

BERTOLO David
Interactions on Digital Tablets in the Context of 3D Geometry Learning
(Human-Machine Interaction Set – Volume 2)

BOUVARD Patricia, SUZANNE Hervé
Collective Intelligence Development in Business

EL FALLAH SEGHROUCHNI Amal, ISHIKAWA Fuyuki, HÉRAULT Laurent, TOKUDA Hideyuki
Enablers for Smart Cities

FABRE Renaud, in collaboration with MESSERSCHMIDT-MARIET Quentin, HOLVOET Margot
New Challenges for Knowledge

GAUDIELLO Ilaria, ZIBETTI Elisabetta
Learning Robotics, with Robotics, by Robotics
(Human-Machine Interaction Set – Volume 3)

HENROTIN Joseph
The Art of War in the Network Age
(Intellectual Technologies Set – Volume 1)

KITAJIMA Munéo
Memory and Action Selection in Human–Machine Interaction
(Human–Machine Interaction Set – Volume 1)

LAGRAÑA Fernando
E-mail and Behavioral Changes: Uses and Misuses of Electronic Communications

LEIGNEL Jean-Louis, UNGARO Thierry, STAAR Adrien
Digital Transformation
(Advances in Information Systems Set – Volume 6)

NOYER Jean-Max
Transformation of Collective Intelligences
(Intellectual Technologies Set – Volume 2)

VENTRE Daniel
Information Warfare – 2nd edition

VITALIS André
The Uncertain Digital Revolution
(Computing and Connected Society Set – Volume 1)

2015

ARDUIN Pierre-Emmanuel, GRUNDSTEIN Michel, ROSENTHAL-SABROUX Camille
Information and Knowledge System
(Advances in Information Systems Set – Volume 2)

BÉRANGER Jérôme
Medical Information Systems Ethics

BRONNER Gérald
Belief and Misbelief Asymmetry on the Internet

IAFRATE Fernando
From Big Data to Smart Data
(Advances in Information Systems Set – Volume 1)

KRICHEN Saoussen, BEN JOUIDA Sihem
Supply Chain Management and its Applications in Computer Science

NEGRE Elsa
Information and Recommender Systems
(Advances in Information Systems Set – Volume 4)

POMEROL Jean-Charles, EPELBOIN Yves, THOURY Claire
MOOCs

SALLES Maryse
Decision-Making and the Information System
(Advances in Information Systems Set – Volume 3)

SAMARA Tarek
ERP and Information Systems: Integration or Disintegration
(Advances in Information Systems Set – Volume 5)

2014

DINET Jérôme
Information Retrieval in Digital Environments

HÉNO Raphaële, CHANDELIER Laure
3D Modeling of Buildings: Outstanding Sites

KEMBELLEC Gérald, CHARTRON Ghislaine, SALEH Imad
Recommender Systems

MATHIAN Hélène, SANDERS Lena
Spatio-temporal Approaches: Geographic Objects and Change Process

PLANTIN Jean-Christophe
Participatory Mapping

VENTRE Daniel
Chinese Cybersecurity and Defense

2013

BERNIK Igor
Cybercrime and Cyberwarfare

CAPET Philippe, DELAVALLADE Thomas
Information Evaluation

LEBRATY Jean-Fabrice, LOBRE-LEBRATY Katia
Crowdsourcing: One Step Beyond

SALLABERRY Christian
Geographical Information Retrieval in Textual Corpora

2012

BUCHER Bénédicte, LE BER Florence
Innovative Software Development in GIS

GAUSSIER Eric, YVON François
Textual Information Access

STOCKINGER Peter
Audiovisual Archives: Digital Text and Discourse Analysis

VENTRE Daniel
Cyber Conflict

2011

BANOS Arnaud, THÉVENIN Thomas
Geographical Information and Urban Transport Systems

DAUPHINÉ André
Fractal Geography

LEMBERGER Pirmin, MOREL Mederic
Managing Complexity of Information Systems

STOCKINGER Peter
Introduction to Audiovisual Archives

STOCKINGER Peter
Digital Audiovisual Archives

VENTRE Daniel
Cyberwar and Information Warfare

2010

BONNET Pierre
Enterprise Data Governance

BRUNET Roger
Sustainable Geography

CARREGA Pierre
Geographical Information and Climatology

CAUVIN Colette, ESCOBAR Francisco, SERRADJ Aziz
Thematic Cartography – 3-volume series
Thematic Cartography and Transformations – Volume 1
Cartography and the Impact of the Quantitative Revolution – Volume 2
New Approaches in Thematic Cartography – Volume 3

LANGLOIS Patrice
Simulation of Complex Systems in GIS

MATHIS Philippe
Graphs and Networks – 2nd edition

THERIAULT Marius, DES ROSIERS François
Modeling Urban Dynamics

2009

BONNET Pierre, DETAVERNIER Jean-Michel, VAUQUIER Dominique
Sustainable IT Architecture: the Progressive Way of Overhauling Information Systems with SOA

PAPY Fabrice
Information Science

RIVARD François, ABOU HARB Georges, MERET Philippe
The Transverse Information System

ROCHE Stéphane, CARON Claude
Organizational Facets of GIS

2008

BRUGNOT Gérard
Spatial Management of Risks

FINKE Gerd
Operations Research and Networks

GUERMOND Yves
Modeling Process in Geography

KANEVSKI Michael
Advanced Mapping of Environmental Data

MANOUVRIER Bernard, LAURENT Ménard
Application Integration: EAI, B2B, BPM and SOA

PAPY Fabrice
Digital Libraries

2007

DOBESCH Hartwig, DUMOLARD Pierre, DYRAS Izabela
Spatial Interpolation for Climate Data

SANDERS Lena
Models in Spatial Analysis

2006

CLIQUET Gérard
Geomarketing

CORNIOU Jean-Pierre
Looking Back and Going Forward in IT

DEVILLERS Rodolphe, JEANSOULIN Robert
Fundamentals of Spatial Data Quality

Printed and bound by CPI Group (UK) Ltd, Croydon, CR0 4YY